Boone

BY *Daniel Firth Griffith*

A Robinia Press Book
VIRGINIA
2020

Edited by Elizabeth Ridgway

A Robinia Press Book

Published By
Robinia Press
530 James River Road
Wingina, Virginia 24599

a division of
Griffith Holdings Inc.
530 James River Road
Wingina, Virginia 24599

Library of Congress
Cataloging-in-Publication Data
Griffith, Daniel, 1993 –
Boone: an Unfinished Portrait / by Daniel Firth Griffith.—1ˢᵗ ed.
p. cm.
Includes bibliographical references.
ISBN-13: 978-1-7354922-2-3

To Morgan, who listened to every story and deleted some of my best sentences.

To Elowyn, who provided the continuous reminder to ask, "Why?"

To Tecumseh, who smiled me through the finish-line.

To Sequoia, whose strength was enough.

TABLE OF

Contents

A NOTE

Concerning Terminology

Many problems exist with any generic or common name for the aboriginal peoples of North America. For the sake of clarity and utilizing the best alternative, I have employed the term "Native" as much as possible, although I am entirely aware of its shortcomings and objections. The peoples that inhabited North America before the European collision were a varied and proud people—true nations in a global sense. Just as there were the English, Dutch, and Spanish, there were the Cherokee, Iroquois, and Shawnee. There were also the Chickahominy, Catawbas, Creeks, Chocktaws, and Chicasas, to name but five of the believed six-hundred distinct nations.

The task of writing frontier ethnohistory is difficult when you are just comparing two opposing cultures, perhaps the French and the English. Enter hundreds of different Nations into the picture and multiply that complexity with the additional intricacy of tribal confederacies, and the resulting story can overwhelm. Whenever possible, I employ each nation's particular name over the term "Native." This is the best alternative, but it again carries its own problems. For example, the Cherokee name was given to them by their invaders—the Europeans. The "Cherokee" people called themselves the Ani-Yunwiya, or, ᎠᏂᏳᏫᏯ, the "Principal People."

In addition, I employ the term "New World" throughout the text, in full understanding that what Christopher Columbus and future "pioneers" understood as "new" was actually very "old." Modern estimates range, but the "New World" was bustling with human life between thirty to forty thousand years ago, a time when Europe was just beginning to crawl. In absence of what I believe to be better alternatives, I employ this terminology to provide clarity to the text—clarity in phraseology that all readers can easily understand and recognize. Only there, at the table of community and reciprocity, can we find healing.

This note exemplifies the need for this text and books like it. Kentucky and the early American West (or the Late West, for that matter) was not an open land for the taking; it was inhabited, peopled, and regenerated itself with its own abundance. Our Western and enlightened mind needs some enlightening by the true West.

Our story is focused on one actor within this historical plane. But the purpose of this work is to use *his* life to highlight the canvas of those around him, especially the natural world, nature-lovers, philosophers, and native peoples. This work is not perfect, as I am not perfect. But it is accurate and I believe it says what it needs to say.

Introduction

The White River Sioux end their prayers with the words, *mitakuya oyasin,* meaning "all my relations." These words are offered as the conclusion of their thanksgiving address and they declare a sense of oneness with the earth, depicting a culture birthed and built from the mythology—maybe even the grammar—of connection and reciprocity.

The Sioux believe in *Takuskanskan,* or, the "mysterious power of motion." It animates that which moves but it also makes motion animate. It pushes and it pulls simultaneously to create movement and out of movement, life. From the wind in our hair to the soul in our bodies, *Takuskanskan* breathes life into all Creation.

In 1967, Jenny Leading Cloud in the White River Rosebud Indian Reservation claimed that "the buffalo and coyote are our brothers; the birds, our cousins," for *Takuskanskan* is in all of us. She continued, "White people see man as nature's master and conqueror, but Indians, who are close to nature, know better." [1] History is the art of "trying to

---

[1] Jenny Leading Cloud. *American Indian Myths and Legends.* Richard Erdoes & Alfonso Ortiz, ed., New York: Pantheon Books, 1984, 5.

know better" and this book is written for those who are ready for the task—to peel back the woods of our very white mythology and discover a history that we may not be entirely comfortable with. The lesson of this story is not progress, but pain, not empire, but empathy. *Takuskanskan.* This story is about motion and life.

. . .

The life of Daniel Boone has been preserved by oral tradition and is riddled with folklore and myth. Although Daniel attempted to record his own story, his autobiography was twice written and twice lost, as his words acted merely as starter agents to many an Native fire. His very name is conspicuous in the annals of history and his legend is known throughout the world, yet few are acquainted with the man and his true character.

Unfortunately, centuries of myth and mist cloud the history of this woodsman. Many presume that Boone was a rugged and coarse backwoodsman, as rough as the wilderness he chased, as savage as the Natives he fought, and as tenacious as the bears he slayed. Contrary to this popular belief, however, he was not the most "rippin'-est, roarin'-est, fightin'-est man the frontier ever knew," to quote the 1960s television series, *Daniel Boone.*

You can also disregard the coonskin hat—he never wore one. The images of Hollywood, presenting him as a gleeful, illiterate hunter of the backcountry wearing nothing but buck and coonskin clothes, are exactly that: images of Hollywood. Boone is most often presented in the muddy mixture of history, legend, and media hysteria as if that picture were real. But such are the powers of man's imagination and modern communications.

Although a household name in both his day and ours, Boone's relationship with his own historical period is often blurred within the popular mind. Geographically, few today know which English colony he called home. Today, the small frontier town of his youth is the fifth largest in the entire state, boasting some eighty-seven thousand residents. In tourist magazines it is referred to as "The Pretzel City," leaving one simple sentence in reference to its founder, Daniel's grandfather. Chronologically, even fewer today can place him alongside his contemporaries with any accuracy. Did he fight alongside George Washington in Braddock's campaign or die defending The Alamo? Your curiosity is not alone, for Daniel himself read many accounts of his own death in local newspapers.

We know the name, but do we know the man? Was he the first to settle the rugged wilderness of Kentucky? Was he the hero of the early American frontier? Was he civilization's pathfinder into the primordial West? Was he an Indian killer? Patriot? American explorer? In her 1985 National Geographic history titled *Daniel Boone: First Hero of the Frontier*, Elizabeth Moize wrote

> Daniel Boone stands as the prototype frontiersman—a strong, silent figure moving swiftly through virgin timber, sighting a deer, felling it with one shot of his flintlock."[2]

---

[2] Moize, Elizabeth A. *Daniel Boone, First Hero of the Frontier.* 1895. 1.

It is his intimate and virgin romance with the land of the setting sun that ignites our dreams and engulfs our folklore. Unequivocally, Boone is the uncontested legend of the early American West. But was he actually legendary?

The majority of the historical information we have of this woodsman is found in manuscripts, early American newspapers, and letters, although over thirty "biographical" volumes have been published on Boone since the late 1780s. These later works offered histories of their own, each either consciously or unconsciously shaping the woodsman's image according to their own predilections, partialities, and predispositions. Therefore, the works produced by Daniel's hunting companions—Peter Houston, Richard Henderson, and Felix Walker, for example—and those produced by Daniel's immediate contacts and family—Nathan Boone, Lyman C Draper, and John Filson—are considered primary sources together with a wide array of newspaper articles, letters, and county documents. Subsequent biographies are treated as extremely useful, but entirely secondary.

While the literary breadth of Daniel Boone is prodigious, its depth is entirely lacking. The obvious deficit of substantial scholarship could be a result of Daniel's private nature. Maybe, perhaps, his biographers found more wealth and animation in his folklore than his fact. However, as the twentieth-century statesman Winston S. Churchill wrote, "The chronicler of ill-recorded times has none the less to tell his tale. If facts are lacking, rumor must serve."[3] In his 1962 Western, *The Man Who Shot Liberty Valance*, director John Ford asserted a similar maxim. Speaking as the editor of the newspaper,

---

[3] Churchill, Winston. *Marlborough: His Life and Times, Book One.* Chicago: Chicago University Press, 1993. 310.

Ford's character, Maxwell Scott, asserted that, in the West, "when the legend becomes fact, print the legend."

The dense atmosphere of the American frontier was incredibly complex. Moreover, it was plagued with paradox. A pioneer and hunter, Daniel Boone epitomized the model of frontier virility and manhood. Although commonly considered the archetypical American frontiersman, a standard-bearer of the American man, Boone's personal understanding of the frontier and its relation to an evolving American regime is anything but clear. Daniel's frontier was the divergent region at the edge of the Anglo-American line of settlement, later known as the American West, although his purpose at the fringe of civilization reveals both a personal and national contradiction.

How is this conflict characterized? As one of the pioneers of civilization's push westwards, Daniel was also the free, independent, and natural man who desired the "simplicity and rugged vitality of the woods beyond all else," writes Boone historian, Michael Lofaro. The more apt his exploration and widespread his reputation, the more available the West became to the modern man. By chasing the sunset to avoid the glare of its rising, Daniel not only paved a physical path but a philosophical map for others to follow. Thus, his destiny appears to be self-defeating, for irony and uncertainty plagued his life and permeated his happiness on the frontier.

Past the conflicting convictions that he confronted, Daniel's character was also complex and composite. Although he was no hermit, Daniel enjoyed the purity of nature and the simplicity of solitude. Although not a lover of civilization, Daniel fought in Braddock's 1755 campaign during the French and Indian War.[4] He also led many men into battle as a Colonel in the United States Militia and he held many civil appointments, including Sheriff and County Lieutenant. Daniel served in the Colony of Transylvania's legislature and then served three terms in the Virginia General Assembly—serving beside Thomas Jefferson in 1781—and established the town of Boonesborough in modern-day Kentucky. For Daniel, the frontier was "simultaneously a challenge and an inspiration, something to subdue and improve as well as to preserve and enjoy."[5]

Early-twentieth-century historian Henry Nash Smith asked in his book, *Virgin Land: The American West as Symbol and Myth*, "Which was the real Boone – the standard-bearer of civilization and refinement, or the child of nature who fled into the wilderness before the advance of settlement?"[6] Was Daniel Boone an empire builder or a philosopher of primitivism? Did a love of—and dedication to—civilization or the untouched and sublime crags of the wilderness urge him forward? *That is the question.*

The man I sought was not in any book or publication; he seemed lost to history. Therefore, I decided to go into history to find the man. White culture has created two Boones, both of them national heroes to be celebrated and revered among names such as David Crocket, John Wayne, and Meriwether Lewis. One speaks for nature; one speaks for empire. This work is a search party to find Daniel Boone and our journey is that of his

[4] Boone, Nathan. *My Father, Daniel Boone: The Draper Interviews with Nathan Boone*. Neal O. Hammon, ed. Lexington: University Press of Kentucky, 1999. 13-14.
[5] Lofaro, Michael A, *Daniel Boone: An American Life*. University of Kentucky Press, 2003. Preface.
[6] Smith, Henry Nash. *Virgin Land: The American West as a Symbol and Myth*. Cambridge: Harvard University Press, 1950. 55.

story's canvas. Although not a comprehensive history, it seeks to find Daniel in *his* woods, with *his* own gun, and with *his* own mind; a goal achieved by first becoming "close to nature," so that we may learn to "know better."

CHAPTER 1

Historiography's Frontier

America's Mythological Enigmas

Before we can enter the living narrative of Daniel's story, I must first indulge myself to enter yours. The undulating American Mind has been shaped by and has even shaped our history, but it has also shaped how our history has been told. Historiography is defined as the study of historical writings and in the literary depths of our past we find the beginnings of this story—our story. To understand Daniel Boone, we must first understand how his story—his history—has been told over the centuries.

Even before his death, Daniel's story befitted the barometer of American consciousness, as his narrative's mythology became clay in the hands of sculptors who eagerly molded his life and values according to their own resident ideals and cultural assumptions. Who was Daniel Boone? He was and is still today a convenient symbol, employed by anyone who thinks they are an American. But what if *he* was not an American? And what if he does not want our employment?

With historiography as the guide, we will peel back Daniel's forest—gently of course, for leaves are fragile and we don't want to disturb that beaver to your left as he creates an ecologically-rich wetland—and attempt to see him as he saw himself. Perhaps, in the naivety and purity of this place, we may also learn something about ourselves. To do both of these things, however, we must first understand the complexity of Daniel's woods.

Historian Daniel J. Boorstin writes in his mid-twentieth century work, *The Lost World of Thomas Jefferson* that, in America, colonizing Europeans were "forced to relive the childhood of their race." As there was no London or Paris in the New World in the sixteenth and seventieth centuries, Boorstin believed that European settlers had to therefore "confront once again the primitive and intractable wilderness of [their] cave-dwelling ancestors."[1] Boorstin's Paleolithic caveman argument carries its own problems—namely, the tremendously racist and deeply anthropocentric belief that highly "cultured" human society is the pinnacle of human activity and that little of such activity existed on the American continent before Columbus.

But his juxtaposition of European civilization and barbarism, between spirituality and savagery paint simply the complex stage of American history and its actors. From the earliest histories written to those that were published when I was in college, the contest of culture over this seemingly wild continent is the central theme of the narrative, although how it is told changes drastically over time, as we will see.

. . . .

---

[1] Boorstin, Daniel. *The Lost World of Thomas Jefferson*, Chicago: University of Chicago Press, 1948. 3.

In his work, *Regeneration Through Violence,* modern cultural critic and historian Richard Slotkin equated the character of a nation to the "intelligible mask" of its mythological "enigmas."[2] Just as we can better understand ancient cultures by looking at their mythology—such as the Vikings and what Valhalla has to tell us about raiding and trading—we can discern the complex worldview of our ancestors and the historical plane on which such views operated by looking at our own mythology.

The perfection of such a study has intrinsic limits, however. The national mythology of the early American frontier exemplifies this natural limit, as the "myth of the frontier"—the "conception of America as a wide-open land of unlimited opportunity for the strong, ambitious, self-reliant individual to thrust his way to the top"—is blind, incomplete, and problematic at best.[3] Yet, from our adolescence, we are taught that America was an open land, ripe and ready for the boisterous youth of its citizenry. Set within this dubious narrative, the American West's historiography pioneered its way through an implacable yet magnificent frontier. To gain a more accurate understanding of the legend and person of Daniel Boone and what that means for us today, we must first understand the nature of this mythology's incessantly evolving relationship with wildness.

---

[2] Slotkin, Richard. *Regeneration Through Violence: The Mythology of the American Frontier, 1600-1860.* Norman: University of Oklahoma Press, 1973. 3.
[3] Slotkin, *Regeneration Through Violence.* 5.

The Analytical, Romantic, and Howling West

Before the emergence of the fundamental Western histories of the late nineteenth century, two strains of frontier history dominated. The first emerged from the accounts and journals of explorers and pioneers and the second from popular images of epic Wild West literature.

During the late colonial and republic periods, explorers such as Meriwether Lewis, Zebulon Pike, William Clark, and Stephen H. Long chronicled their journeys west with furnishings of flora and fauna, of terrains and native peoples. If one were to crack open the analytical *Journal of Lewis and Clark* or *The Expeditions of Zebulon Montgomery Pike to Headwaters of the Mississippi River* they would find riveting descriptions of Western flora and fauna.

After measuring the confluence of the Missouri and Yellowstone rivers (which were 520 yard and 858 yards wide respectively), Lewis wrote that he "walked on shore with one man about 8 A.M." After a short walk, Lewis shoots a brown or yellow or white bear—for some reason this is unclear—and goes on to estimate its weight (about 300 pounds), for, as he notes, they did "not hav[e] the means for ascertaining it precisely."[4] On the seventh of November, 1805, Lewis journals that, after a "cloudy [and] foggey morning [with] some rain," their camp is "in view of the Ocian this great Pacific Ocian which we been so long anxious to see." Although they technically did not reach the Pacific until a good number of days later—they made it to the bay, not the ocean—their exuberance at a three-year and simply exhausting journey was simply

---

[4] *Journals of Lewis and Clark*, Frank Bergon, ed., New York: Penguin Group, 1989. 110.

described with the note that there "was great joy in camp."[5] As I said, riveting.

Although these accounts were undoubtedly spurred by the politics of the day, they also were decidedly scientific and carried other purposes such as observation and documentation. On the seventh of September, 1803, William Clark provided the first European description of a coyote, calling these mystical fox-like wolves, "borrowing rats." Days later, after he had "killed [one] about the size of a grey fox," he cemented on calling them the "prairie wolff."[6] Earlier that year, President Thomas Jefferson provided instructions to Captain Meriwether Lewis that speak to the partially scientific founding of this mission

> Other objects worthy of notice will be, the soil and face of the country, its growth and vegetable productions, especially those not of the United States, the animals of the country generally, and especially those not known in the United States; the remains and accounts of any which may be deemed rare or extinct; the mineral productions of every kind, but particularly metals, limestone, pit-coal and saltpeter.

To Jefferson's credit, he urged Lewis that "in all your intercourse with the natives treat them in the most friendly & conciliatory manner," although Jefferson qualified the motive

---

[5] *Journals of Lewis and Clark*, Frank Bergon, ed., 316.
[6] *Journals of Lewis and Clark*, Frank Bergon, ed., 50.

of this encouragement was to provide "some security of your own party."[7]

Properly titled as journals or accounts, these historical narratives focused on the American West as a perilous but picturesque land; a living and breathing frontier that needed documenting and mapping, not necessarily conquering and civilizing. Left out of such organic memoirs were the imaginative reshapings of their experiences that later frontier writers so deftly employed. They were not romantic; they were real. Sometimes, too real.

It was not until the mid-to-late nineteenth century that literary images of romance beyond the line of Anglo-American settlement became embedded in Western history and literature. Although authors such as Washington Irving took "copious factual notes" of the West and studied the early and analytical journals of Western explorers, Irving fashioned his work by separating the East from the West—society from savagery. Irving's West was passionate, but his wilderness made "explicit the social distinctions between his unpolished frontiersmen and their sophisticated Eastern companions."[8] It was the thrill of the chase, the nighttime escapades of forbidden lovers, and the clash of cultures that saturated the romantic rhythm of this period.

James Fenimore Cooper contributed much to this second epoch of American frontier history. Cooper later admitted that many of his frontier characters and narratives were derived from the many legends of Daniel Boone. In his books—

---

[7] *The Papers of Thomas Jefferson*, vol. 40, *4 March–10 July 1803*, ed. Barbara B. Oberg. Princeton: Princeton University Press, 2013, 176–183.

[8] Etulain, Richard W. "Introduction: The Rise of Western Historiography," in *Writing Western History: Essays on Major Western Historians*. ed., Richard W. Etulain. Albuquerque: University of New Mexico Press, 1991. 2.

Pathfinder, The Pioneers, The Deerslayer, Prairie, and *The Last of the Mohicans*—Cooper utilizes the figures of Leatherstocking, Natty Bumppo, and Trapper as the "personification of strength, courage," and "responsibility" that Daniel Boone embodied in American history.[9] The moral foundations of Cooper's heroes were instilled by the workings of nature and unsullied solitude rather than the proper yet impractical hand of civilization. So depicted, American heroes were rooted in soil, not society, and the explorer as hunter and Indian fighter began to permeate, animate, and romance American mythology.

Taken as historical accounts, these works were little better than illustrations of European ethnocentrism masked in a frontier façade. They were written by outsiders, a West beheld by both the spectacle and scruples of the East. Cooper himself was born in Burlington, New Jersey. Although such tableaux, from Irving to Cooper, exhibit no single or definite focus, they all share one notable characteristic. Historian Richard Etulian writes that the shared quality of this period was

> An ambivalence that *cherished* the open landscape and freedom of the West on the one hand but *hesitated* to embrace the frontier characters and sociocultural life on the other.[10]

---

[9] Morgan, Robert. *Boone: A Biography.* Chapel Hill: Algonquin Books of Chapel Hill, 2007. Niles' Register, X, 361 (June 15, 1816). 447; Kolodny, Annette. *The Land Before Her: Fantasy and Experience of the American Frontiers, 1630-1860.* Chapel Hill: The University of North Carolina Press, 1984. 28.

[10] Etulain, Richard W. "Introduction: The Rise of Western Historiography," in *Writing Western History: Essays on Major Western Historians.* ed., Richard W. Etulain. Albuquerque: University of New Mexico Press, 1991. 3.

Their West was a marvel to behold on museum walls; a West to spark romantic imagination on civilization's wooded periphery. Cooper's first book, *Precaution,* is popularly believed to have been influenced not by the rushing rivers of the interior of this harsh continent but the English writings of Jane Austin. Most importantly, their West was not *the* American West, although beautifully comparable to the fictional lands of Lilliput or Valhalla.

Timothy Flint's 1833 *Biographical Memoir of Daniel Boone* exemplifies this romantically quixotic depiction. Writing of Boone's travels in the Kentucky wilderness, Flint asserted

> No feeling, but a devotion to their favorite pursuits and modes of life, stronger than the fear of abandonment, in the interminable and pathless woods, to all forms of misery and death, could ever have enabled them to persist in braving the danger and distress that stared them in the face at every advancing step.[11]

Flint's wilderness was the grand opening stage in the providential play of civilization and Boone's role was its triumphant leader. Possessing minor historical authority, Flint's work displayed his idealistic Western-ism. In his introduction to Flint's biography, James K. Folsom concluded that, to Flint, "life in the West becomes more desirable as conditions in the West itself approach conditions in the East."

Flint's portrait although telling is not unique. In his 1845 biography, *Daniel Boone—The First Hunter of Kentucky,*

---

[11] Flint, Timothy, *Biographical Memoir of Daniel Boone,* ed. James K Folsom. New Haven: Yale University Press, 1967. 46.

William Gilmore Simms presented Boone as a "knight errant," driven by aristocratic heroism and virtue and not afraid to challenge the primitive Indian in a duel of the mind or the bout.[12] Such romantically progressive and action-oriented histories presented Boone as the Columbus of the wilderness, determined to chart the un-chartable and pacify the recalcitrant barbarian. He was civilization's omnipotent pathfinder, leading God's holy mission in the New World not with a holy staff but with a punishing stick.

But Wild West histories emerged long before the nineteenth century, although their focus concentrated on general human affairs and not necessarily Daniel Boone. The New England Puritans of the early seventeenth century were intent on building a new Zion in America. Unlike later migrants who risked the Atlantic's perilous journey for increased wealth or freedom, the Puritans of Massachusetts were driven by devotion, chastity, and their family's spiritual condition—a striking seventy percent came over with in-tact families with them.[13] In many ways, it was the ruggedness of the journey itself that purified the social chaff from Abraham's seed—a collective winnowing of their ranks.

This deep religious impulse motivated both their migration and their mission. One early Puritan transplant, John Dane, explained that his migration was incited by the idea that "I should be more free here than [in Europe] from temptations,"

---

[12] William Gilmore Simms, "Daniel Boone—The First Hunter of Kentucky," in his *Views and Reviews in American Literature, History and Fiction,* ed. C. Hugh Holman (1845; reprint, Cambridge: Belknap Press of Harvard University, 1963), pp. 149-51.
[13] Fischer, David Hacket, *Albion's Seed: Four British Folkways in America.* New York: Oxford University Press, 1989. 25.

for, in the New World, he would "touch no unclean thing."[14] Secular society did not dominate in New England. We need only to look at the Massachusetts Bay Company's great seal to understand that the Puritan mission was not altogether pure itself. Standing naked and passive, with only a few leaves covering its body and its arms outstretched, a native begs for help. English words flow from its mouth that read, "Come over and help us." Perhaps this derogatory image paints a very different picture of John Winthrop's appeal that "we shall be as a City upon a Hill, the eyes of all people are upon us."[15] At least he called them people.

Although less than ten percent of emigrating Puritans came from a European metropolis, their literature and histories once in the New World paint their wooded periphery as a devilish wasteland, howling and filled with barbarous Indians. The cultural and geographic heritage of these migrants provides interesting study, as the majority of them came from East Anglia and surrounding locales. Historically, these lands in the seventeenth century tended to be "flat, open country, with long vistas of unbroken views of the sky."[16] At the same time, however, the populations of East Anglia have long been exposed to sea-based hazards in the form of raiders and marauders. As late as 1626, just six years after the first Puritans landed in New England, the inhabitants of East Anglia defended their coast from the dreaded "Dunkirkers" who "came ashore killing, looting, and raping."[17]

---

[14] John Dane, "A Declaration of Remarkabell Prouidenses in the Corse of My Lyfe," NEHGR 8 (1854).
[15] John Winthrop, "A Modell of Christian Charity Written on Board the Arrabella on the Atlantick Ocean," *Winthrop Papers,* II, 282.
[16] Fischer, David Hacket, *Albion's Seed.* 42.
[17] Fischer, David Hacket, *Albion's Seed.* 44.

In their new Zion, the Puritans faced an altogether new problem. They were the sea-born raiders and their conquered fields were currently shaded by a great canopy of trees. They came to the new world to escape temptation but discovered temptation itself. Unlike the mythical analogue of John Bunyan's *Pilgrim's Progress,* where the model Christian departs on a heroic quest not as a conquering commander but as a simple figure seeking repose from a sinful humanity, the Puritan's quest into New England's frontier discovered a world altogether unchristian and altogether their own.

The temptations of truculence were at their doorstep and they understood that the aggressive root was the Native—a half-naked insignia of barbarism—and their dense wilderness as its source. What did they do? They conserved their culture of religious piety by plainly pitting it up against a world antithetical to their own. By accentuating their own spiritual enlightenment, they could distance the barbarism at their doorstep. Richard Slotkin concluded

> The basic factors in the physical and psychological situation of the colonists were the wildness of the land, its blending of unmitigated harshness and tremendous potential fertility; the absence of strong European cultures on the borders; and the eternal presence of the native people of the woods, dark of skin and seemingly dark of mind, mysterious, bloody, cruel, "devil-worshipping."[18]

In his 1662 address, *God's Controversy with New England,* seventeenth-century Puritan Minister Michael

---

[18] Slotkin, *Regeneration Through Violence.* 18.

Wigglesworth aptly described the tone of the Puritan attitude toward the frontier. As one of the first settlers of New England, Wigglesworth was both a minister and professor. A very strict Puritan, perhaps due to the potentially morbid state of mind that life-long bodily weakness and chronic health issues can produce, Wigglesworth believed that any pleasure derived from outside of the simple satisfaction found within God's grace was unwarrantable. In June of 1653 he witnessed some of his students at Harvard indulging in merriment, wherein he wrote,

> But still I see the Lord shutting out my prayers and refusing to hear for he whom in special I pray'd for, I heard in the forenoon with ill company playing musick, though I had so solemnly warn'd him but yesterday of letting his spirit go after pleasures.

Wigglesworth's zeal for perfect piety was not unfounded, however. The Puritan attitude focused on community obedience that was only obtainable if all members of the community cooperated in universal vigilance.

In his 1662 address, Wigglesworth described the American West as "a waste and howling wilderness, where none inhabited but hellish fiends, and brutish men that devils worshiped."[19] In this devils' den, he equated the rugged wilderness of the frontier with that of hell and its inhabitants as "fiends" unfit for human society and unwelcome in human civilization. Wigglesworth's depiction transformed the depths of the Ohio and the heights of the Alleghenies into an

---

[19] Wigglesworth, Michael. "God's Controversy with New England," in Proceedings of the Massachusetts Historical Society, XII (1871-1873), 83, 84. (1662)

impenetrable wall that blocked the savagery of the West from corrupting the purified East. In a sense, he credited the New World's topography as the buffering handiwork of their Creator.

Such early American frontier ideology was chronicled in dramatized accounts of hunter heroes and innocent maidens escaping from their barbarian captives, overcoming a remote wilderness infested with savages. Presented as histories, these "captivity narratives," as they are called, praised the triumphant hero for their chastity, Christianity, and courage among their captives. In his introduction to *Writing Western History: Essays on Major Western Historians,* Richard W. Etulian summarized the core of these narratives

> Since the West was less advanced than the East, it needed civilizing agents, and progress dictated that less advanced people and ideologies must give way to higher laws of progress and civilization. The West was truly wild—in need of giant doses of society and culture, which the East alone could provide.[20]

This early ideology illustrated the American West as a territory that needed saving—a saving possible only through a cascade of cathedrals and of heroes. Slotkin claimed this mythology "embodied the dark side of the Puritan attitude toward the natural world in general and toward the American wilderness in particular."[21]

Although the potency of captivity narratives and their resulting myths remained strong, American mythology's focus again shifted in the beginning of the eighteenth century. Its

---

[20] Etulain, *Writing Western History: Essays on Major Western Historians.* 4.
[21] Slotkin, *Regeneration Through Violence.* 146.

revised tone exchanged the howling wilderness with a more representative recognition of the frontier as restorative and engaging. Benjamin Church's 1716 publication, *Entertaining Passages Relating to Philip's War*, marks the literary shift of this new and more-realistic, but still entirely fabricated, mythology. In his adventurous accounts, Church employed the strength and heroism of the woodland hunter in place of the pious and hapless victim. He presented the wilderness as habitable—a place for only the truly American.

Church's hunter-hero bridged the gap between the new and the archetypal American; it fostered both security and homeliness within the wooded periphery and formed a "manual of information about the Indians...not a religious tract anathematizing them," writes Etulian.[22] This shift, the revision of the role of the Native in American affairs, laid the definitional groundwork of what we understand today as the "representative American"—a hunter-hero that was both European and American; both decidedly civilized and entirely natural.

Enter John Filson's 1784 portrayal of Daniel Boone. Presenting him as the archetypal yet ironic American frontier-hero, who was "the lover of the spirit of the wilderness...with acts of love and sacred affirmation [as] acts of violence against that spirit and her avatars," Filson depicted Boone's entrance into manhood as a baptism by battle. Just as the Puritan's strength required continual affirmations of their "Englishness" and Church's wilderness demanded the strength and resolve of the hunter-hero, Boone's struggles to address this muddled dividing required a decisive dependence on the sword—or, in his case, the gun. The mythological shift is apparent against

---

[22] Etulain, *Writing Western History: Essays on Major Western Historians.* 181.

Boone's received worldview. Filson's Boone is the arbitrator between society and savagery and stands on the pedestal of the secularly based, deeply rationalistic, and "manly" philosophy of the frontier.

One author of this period attempted to combine the mythology of both Church and Filson into one narrative. In 1786, John Trumbull published a pirated version of Filson's narrative, removing the philosophy in the original text to focus on Boone as a man of action. Trumbull also bound this new work with the captivity narrative of Mrs. Frances Scott, a woman victimized by the ferocious barbarians and their wilderness. In this new combination of romantic mythology, with the hero and the captive in one volume, Trumbull pinned the conquest *of* the wilderness and the victimization *by* the wilderness against each other. The hero of the Indian war stepped in to rescue the maiden of the captivity narratives. Trumbull's work, built on the hunter-hero-maiden paradox, presents the West as both hopeful and howling; both realistic and idealistic.

The Revised West and Progressive Historicism

By the late nineteenth century, the old West was the new East, and the focus of American mythology was refit for its new geography. California was now a state, no longer an idea, and the Rockies were not impenetrable walls, but mountable territories, primed for profit and pleasure. The works of Frederick Jackson Turner define this new era in American Western historiography.

Governed not by "laws of man's devising," Turner's Western victors were a part of the "moral order of the universe, ruled by cosmic forces from above," writes German Philosopher Frederick Schelling.[23] Driven by natural philosophy and folk democracy, Turner's work depicted the pioneers' path through the Cumberland Gap as though it was down the triumphant streets of Rome and the sweat on their brows as though it was the laurel upon their head. Turner's model grew to dominate American mythology and supplied a substantial primer to the modern historian.

Turner seemingly desired to renovate the study of American history, including a more concentrated gaze on the "large role the frontier had played in shaping the American past," illuminating the causes of national thought and politics.[24] At this point in American history, the United States had defended its independence and unity on three different occasions and had graduated from an idea to an empire. "The real lines of American development, the forces dominating our character," writes Turner, "are to be studied in the history of Western expansion."[25] Understanding the West was the key to understanding America. He believed that we must look past the memories and narratives of heroes to discover the "deeper" and broader "forces" that fashioned American uniqueness and he strove to write a truly democratic history, focused on the Far West as the "physiographic province itself decreed that the

---

[23] Noble, David W. "Frederick Jackson Turner: The Machine and the Loss of the Covenant" in *Historians Against History: The Frontier Thesis and the National Covenant in American Historical Writing since 1830.* Minneapolis: University of Minnesota Press, 1965. 41.

[24] Billington, Ray. *Frederick Jackson Turner Historian, Scholar, Teacher* (New York: Oxford University Press, 1973).

[25] Turner, Frederick Jackson. "Problems in American History," *The Aegis,* November 4, 1892, repr. in *Early Writings, 72.*

destiny of this new frontier should be social rather than individual."[26]

Although writing at the turn of the twentieth century, Turner believed that "the story of the peopling of America [had] not yet been written. We do not understand ourselves," he claimed.[27] By transforming history from a discipline akin to literature to that of social science, however, Turner's philosophical idealism was extraordinarily relativistic. Historian William Cronon argued

> [Turner's model] pointed the way toward the pragmatic epistemological stance that would so characterize American progressive thought. Turner was nothing if not a progressive. The specific historical agenda he urged on his listeners had all the earmarks of an early, optimistic progressivism—just as his own argument predicted it would. ...[Turner's] story...was ultimately about evolution, a progressive narrative about the sequential stages of social growth that mimicked what Darwin had discovered in biology.[28]

Turner's progressivism colored his analytical essays and histories as well as his romantic poems. In his May, 1883 poem, *The Poet of the Future,* Turner claimed that the future poet

> will find beauty in the useful and the common. ...In his ear humanity will whisper deep, inspiring words, and bid him

---

[26] Turner, Frederick Jackson. "Contributions of the West to American Democracy," in *Frontier in American History.* 258.

[27] *Frontier and Section: Selected Essays of Frederick Jackson Turner.* ed., Ray Allen Billington. (Englewood Cliffs, N.J.: Prentice-Hall, 1961), 25.

[28] *Frontier and Section: Selected Essays of Frederick Jackson Turner.* 75.

give them voice. He will unite the logic of the present and the dream of the past, and his words will ring in the ears of generations yet unborn, telling them the grandeur of today which boils and surges with awakening life. He will reflect all the past and prophesy the future.

There is an unhindered flow of events—an inevitable progressivism —in Turner's thought. It is the "logic" of the present that "boils and surges with awakening life," while the incomplete past merely dreams.

In accordance with Darwinian evolution, the broad progress of humanity—and its historiography—always flows from barbarism to civilization, from "dreams" to "logic." In his essay titled *The Frontier and American Institutions,* George Wilson Pierson concluded that Turner thought of the frontier "primarily in terms of nature, of geography, of physical environment."[29] Pierson termed such a hypothesis as a "kind of geographic or environmental determinism."

One illustration of this is Turner's "trading post." As the meeting ground of the primitive and the advanced, the Western fur trade and subsequent trading post acted as the connection point and "transforming force" of Western society, wrote Turner.[30] As though a perfectly choreographed play, the trading post served as the stage of cultural and social evolution, while its actors—progressing from pioneers and Indians to that

[29] Pierson, George Wilson. "The Frontier and American Institutions: A Criticism of the Turner Theory," in *The Turner Thesis: Concerning the Role of the Frontier in American History.* ed., George Rogers Taylor. Lexington: D. C. Heath and Company, 1972. 74.
[30] Turner, Frederick Jackson. *The Character and Influence of the Indian Trade in Wisconsin.* 3-5, 18, 19.

of colonists and yeoman—became the "pathfinder[s] for civilization."[31]

Understanding the primitive as a germ to be developed and cultured—maybe even educated—Turner applauded civilization's effects on the West. His providential veneer praised the drifting backwoodsman who "found too little elbow room in town life" yet he exalted "the spirit of the pioneer's 'house raising.'" [32] The desire for open land and the need for community, Turner claimed, was "salvation of the Republic."[33] The geographic dominance of undeveloped space to be ultimately conquered by the township was the foundation of American republicanism—the Frenchmen Alexis de Tocqueville also perceived the force of the American township. Turner concluded his *Rise of the New West, 1819-1829* with valiance: "and on the frontier of the northwest, the young Abe Lincoln sank his axe deep in the opposing forest."[34]

Enter the 1922 Boy Scouts of America publication, *Daniel Boone, Wilderness Scout*. Not five hundred words into the book, Stewart Edward White argues that, "it did not matter what especial deeds [the American pioneers] performed." Rather, their "deeds became renowned ... because of the men who did them."[35] White's focus was on forming an American character, not on the truthful examination of the characters of

---

[31] Turner, *The Character and Influence of the Indian Trade in Wisconsin.* 19.

[32] Turner, Frederick Jackson. "Hunter Type," in Jacobs, ed., *Frederick Jackson Turner's Legacy,* 153, and "Middle Western Pioneer Democracy," in *Frontier in American History,* 358.

[33] Turner, *Frederick Jackson Turner's Legacy,* 153; "Middle Western Pioneer Democracy," in *Frontier in American History,* 358.

[34] Turner, Frederick Jackson. *Rise of the New West: 1819-1829* (New York: Harper and Brothers, 1906), 332.

[35] White, Stewart Edward, *Daniel Boone Wilderness Scout.* New York: Doubleday & Company, Inc, 1922. 5-6.

America. Accordingly, stalwart heroes of the frontier defined the American exceptionalism that would later transform the West from savage to sophisticated. It is this very American history that connected Daniel Boone to the "discovery" of Kentucky—it is because of what he represented, not because he discovered it. That is immaterial. The point is flow, not accuracy. White declared

> [Boone] was one of the many great Indian fighters of his time; lived for years with his rifle and tomahawk next his hand; lost brothers and sons under the scalping knife. He was a master of woodcraft, able to find his way hundreds of miles through unbroken forests, able to maintain himself alone not merely for a day or a week but for a year or more without other resources than his rifle, his tomahawk, and his knife; and this in the face of the most wily foes. He was muscular and strong and enduring; victor in many a hand-to-hand combat, conqueror of farms cut from the forest; performer of long journeys afoot at speeds that would seem incredible to a college athlete. He was a dead shot with a rifle, an expert hunter of game.

In other words, Daniel Boone was the standard that all valiant Boy Scouts should live up to—the pole bearer of American youth. He was, in many ways, the Scout of Scouts.

Although Turner's thesis on Western history revolutionized American historiography—seen even today when the chapters of modern textbooks advance in their discussion of Western history from *Indians* to *explorers* to *farmers*—his construction of social evolution was at its core deeply problematic, for it interpreted the past in light of modern events. In her 1987 book, *The Legacy of Conquest,* Patricia Limerick writes that the true images of the American frontier—the broad plains, rushing rivers, and high mountains—never "found much of a home in [Turner's historical] model."[36] Turner's frontier was, simply, a creation, an idea of the thing rather than the thing itself, and produced its own variety of American thought.

In his main thesis, *The Significance of History,* Turner wrote that each age "writes the history of the past anew" and with "a different ideal of history." His words reverberate with a sense of historicism that replaces rational judgment with transient historical context. In objection to a later form of such a potentially erred reasoning, the twentieth-century political philosopher, writer, and University of Chicago professor Leo Strauss wrote that historicism "imposes" a "single comprehensive view…on us by fate: the horizon within which all our understanding and orientation take place is produced by the fate of the individual or of his society."[37] Turner's thesis eradicated both natural right and justice in the realm of political order, leaving its actors on the complex stage of American history forever unknown and invariably worthless.

But Turner's thesis is not without worth, however. The idea that history repeats itself—that the eighteenth-century history of the Cumberland Gab would also become the nineteenth-century history of Wyoming's South Pass—is painfully true. The complex pillars of human action are decently

---

[36] Limerick, Patricia Nelson. *Legacy of Conquest: The Unbroken Past of The American West.* New York: W.W. Norton & Company, 1987. 21.
[37] Strauss, Leo. *Natural Right and History.* Chicago: University of Chicago Press, 1953. 27.

steady throughout history, although their telling of such history, according to Turner, should differ greatly.

Regardless of its intention, Turner's work begs Western historians to question whether American mythology should center on particular frontier experiences or on the broad and universal field of human action. Can aristocratic histories be written of democratic heroes? Should efforts be directed to consider individual action or universal progress? More particularly, for our story, how was it that a backcountry woodsman became an American cultural icon?

With attentions directed by classical antiquity, however, the writings of Plutarch and Thucydides, of Xenophon and Homer tell us where to focus our efforts: at both heroes and their regimes and at particular actions and universal principles. It was Xenophon's history of Cyrus the Great that illustrated the universal prudence of understanding human nature; Homer's Achilles that illustrated pride, grief, and heroism within the ancient Greek world; and Thucydides' Pericles—that orated "to be happy means to be free, and to be free means to be brave"— that illustrated the universal axioms of a democratic regime based in freedom and human virtue.

The answer appears clear: it is through the mountain pass of both human thought and action that the bedrock of human nature and the resulting political institutions are best understood; it is in the unifying of both history and poetry, of the particulars and the universals, that the true and objective life of Daniel Boone can be unveiled. So positioned, perhaps, he can even speak to us—if we listen.

CHAPTER 2

Curiosity is Natural

Of Wanderlust and Beginnings

Born in the frontier town of Oley, Pennsylvania, on October 22, 1734, Daniel was the son of restless and dissenting Quaker immigrants.[38] Named after his mother's brother, Reverend Daniel Morgan, or perhaps, the notable Dutch painter—also named Daniel Boone—who was believed to be a distant relative, our Daniel grew up on the Western edge of European settlement. Unlike either of his namesakes, however, he was neither a reverend nor a painter—he was a woodsman.

Daniel was born into a pious and pacifistic world crafted a century earlier by war. Although the English Civil Wars of the mid-seventeenth century established the precedent of Parliamentary consent—meaning that the English monarch could not govern without the backing of its Parliament—and commenced the decade-long military dictatorship led by Oliver Cromwell, their durable impact within our story was religious, rather than governmental.

The English Civil Wars forced Charles I off the throne and his head off his shoulders. The Church of England was also dethroned in the aftermath. During the post-war era, many

---

[38] Boone, *My Father, Daniel Boone: The Draper Interviews with Nathan Boone.* 10.

influential and increasingly radical religious sects fermented in the relative freedom and toleration of the new English crock. Among such were the Quakers—or the Society of Friends. Founded by George Fox, the son of a Puritan weaver, the Quaker faith emerged in 1647 out of Fox's distaste for the Church of England.[39] Believing in the equality of the sexes, relative pacifism, and that direct experience with Christ was possible outside of the ordained clergy—that, simply, "the Lord is come to teach his people *himself* by his grace, light, truth, and Spirit"—Fox's faith quickly spread across England and its budding New World.[40]

In 1681, William Penn's tolerant and free colony of Pennsylvania was founded to harbor the Quakers alongside many other dissenting religious groups and peoples, namely the Dutch, Swedish, and English. In his late-seventeenth-century publication, *The Great Case of the Liberty of Conscience,* Penn argued that, by "Liberty of Conscience," he sought not "only a meer Liberty of the Mind," but the "exercise of ourselves" in religion. Literally named "Penn's Woods," Pennsylvania's rugged frontier offered more than political refuge and matchless economic opportunity. It offered a religious sanctuary never before seen in modern Europe. Not only could man believe what his conscience dictated, but he could freely practice the dictates of his conscience. In this sense, the wilderness and isolation of the New World secured man's right to "the most sacred of all property"—his conscience.[41] With thought and action so

---

[39] Tindall, George Brown and Shi, David E, "Settling The Middle Colonies and Georgia," *in America, A Narrative History* (New York: W. W. Norton & Company, 2004), Volume I: 88.

[40] Fox, George. *A Journal of the Life, Travels, Sufferings, Christian Experiences, and Labour of Love of George Fox.* William Armistad, ed. Glascow: W.G. Balckie & Co., 197.

[41] Madison, James, "Property," in *50 Core American Documents,* pg 94.

wedded, the confluence of the Schuylkill and Delaware Rivers quickly grew into a hub of brotherly love, economic trade, and religious toleration—the City of Philadelphia. By 1685, William Penn had sold over 700,000 acres of land, half of which was to Quaker settlers.[42]

In Penn's Quaker-galvanized and free woods, relations with the American native were surprisingly pleasant. The Seneca Indians even gave Penn a name, "Onas," meaing quill or pen.[43] One history of this period wrote that "the settlers and the natives lived side by side in peace" and held such trust in the amicability in their relations that "that Quaker farmers sometimes left their children in the care of Indians when they were away from home."[44] In his first letter to the Delawares in 1681, Penn conveyed his intent on "true friendship" and declared that he wanted to "winn and gain their love and friendship by a kind, just and peaceable life" through both sobriety and kindness.[45]

The Quakers, more broadly, also desired the same. They wished to create a world where "the wolf may lie down with the lamb and the lion with the calf," although it is unclear who they thought they were in this analogy. In a sense, the Quakers of the New World transformed their "swords into plowshares" and their "spears into pruning hooks," to borrow

---

[42] Jean R. Soderlund, ed., *William Penn and the Founding of Pennsylvania, 1680-1684* (Philadelphia: University of Pennsylvania Press, 1983), 5.
[43] McClure, David, *Diary of David McClure*. New York: The Knickerbocker Press, 1899. 65.
[44] Tindall, George Brown and Shi, David E, "Settling The Middle Colonies and Georgia," 90.
[45] Dunn, Richard and Dunn, Mary Maples, "Letter from William Penn to the King of the Indians," in The Papers of William Penn, 5 vols. (Philadelphia: University of Pennsylvania Press, 1981-86), 128-129.

the language of Penn.[46] They were a rugged, independent, and capable people intent on bringing "things back into their primitive and right order again."[47]

The Boone family was cast from the same mold. George Boone, Daniel's grandfather, converted to Quakerism around 1702. He was a respected weaver of an old English family—dating back at least two centuries—in the village of Bradninch in Southwest England. In 1713, George sent his two sons, Squire and George, and their sister, Sarah, to Pennsylvania to ascertain the truth of William Penn's "liberty of conscience." They were to act as family pathfinders—*pioneers*—and relay their findings back to him. The new land and liberty seemed to please them, for, upon Squire's beckoning on August 17, 1717, George Boone removed his family from Devon's serene meadows—remembered as "one of the most beautiful counties of Great Britain, a place of highland and moors covered with heather and bracken, high rocky hills, long pleasant valleys running down to the sea"—and sailed for the New World's wild and unknown frontiers.[48]

This migration was not unique, however. While most Boone historians cast the Boone family's emigration to the new world as a plain indication of their seemingly genetic wanderlust, it appears that nearly a quarter million others shared their wanderlust at the same time and five thousand annually until the American Revolution. During the summer of 1717, the Delaware river was overwhelmed with incoming immigrant vessels and Johnathan Dickinson, a resident of Philadelphia and an ardent Quaker, complained that the streets teemed with "a

---

[46] Penn, William, "For of Light Came Sight," in *The Quaker Reader*, Wallingford: Pendle Hill Publications, 1962. 110.
[47] Penn, William, *The Quaker Reader*. 113.
[48] Morgan, *Boone: A Biography*. 1.

swarm of people ... strangers in our Laws and Customs, and even to our language."[49] This should neither discredit the Boones desires nor discount their seemingly innate passion for the frontier and disposition towards restlessness, but simply act as a minor temper to the historical narrative. Yes, the Boones were an "adventurous breed" and "wanderer's born," as one early Boone historian notes, but so were many of this era.[50]

A weaver by trade, Squire was a man of enterprise and strength. On December 3, 1728, he bought a favorable tract of one hundred and forty-seven acres in New Britain Township, Bucks County. In characteristic Boone fashion, Squire again expanded his land holdings in 1730 with an adjoining two-hundred-and-fifty-acre tract in Oley Township.[51] His land was remembered as a "beautiful, gently rolling country covered by hardwood forests that opened to grassy meadows."[52]

Squire employed his land for farming, his hand for blacksmithing and weaving, and his mind for local government.[53] Self-reliant, patient and full of common sense, Squire was well suited for frontier life. He was a characteristic Boone: small statured, but "touched with restlessness, curiosity, an urge to move on."[54] He appears to also have been a well-tempered man, with curiosity always checked by caution. Whenever possible, Squire would "consider, ponder, reconnoiter," and examine the ground around him.[55]

[49] Jonathan Dickinson to Cousin, 17 Oct 1719, Jonathan Dickinson Letterbook, 1715-21, HSP.
[50] Morgan, *Boone: A Biography*. Chapter 1.
[51] Modern day Berks County, PA.
[52] Faragher, *Daniel Boone: the Life and Legend of an American Pioneer*. 10.
[53] Bakeless, *Daniel Boone: Master of the Wilderness*. 7; Lofaro, *Daniel Boone: An American Life*. 2.
[54] Bakeless, *Daniel Boone*. 3.
[55] Bakeless, *Daniel Boone*. 4.

John Bakeless, Daniel Boone's first definitive biographer,[56] wrote in his book, *Daniel Boone: Master of the Wilderness*

> [the Boones] had the itching foot. Something called. Something beyond the mountains always whispered. They heard the distant lands and knew that they must go there."[57]

Upon Thomas Jefferys' 1776 *Map of Pennsylvania*, "Boone's Mill" rested in the picturesque Schuylkill River Valley, across from the "Quaker Meeting House" and on the main public road that connected the increasingly populated center of Philadelphia with the frontier town of Tulpehocken.[58] Oley, the town built around this road and the town of Daniel's youth, is an Algonquian word meaning "valley." Both near civilization and its border regions, the Boone settlement was a physical depiction of their historical reality: forever torn between white and native culture, between the civilized and the primitive. Their cultural heritage may have been from distant lands, but their future was something entirely natural—and increasingly native.

Although often remembered for his father's restless curiosity and wanderlust, Daniel was his mother's son. Sarah Morgan married Squire Boone on July 23, 1720. She was described by her great-nephew, Daniel Bryan, as "over the common size, strong and active, with black hair and eyes, and raised in the Quaker order." She was also considered "well

---

[56] Opinion of Lofaro, *Daniel Boone: An American Life.* 2.
[57] Bakeless, *Daniel Boone.* 5.
[58] "Oley" is the Algonquian word for valley.

calculated" like her husband.[59] Sarah's father, Edward Morgan of Bala, sailed for the New World in 1691 and settled with his family in the Moyamensing District of Philadelphia.

They were descendants from the ancient Morgans of Merionethshire, a place with topography most renowned "for its mountain crags and mists" and, as the early twelfth century historian and priest Giraldus Cambrensis wrote, is most often considered as "the roughest and rudest of all the Welsh districts." The ancient Morgans were an isolated, rugged, but not impetuous people, lovers of liberty who preferred peace and happiness on "their own terms and in their own rugged world."[60] In a sense, they were jealous of their liberty and sincere in their fidelity. In as much as topography can make a man—a science today understood as epigenetics—the Morgan family line was hewn from rough and unique conditions.

Sarah was no different. Nathan Boone, Daniel's youngest son, in a 1851 interview with Lyman Draper, described his grandmother as "a woman of great neatness and industry."[61] Peter Houston, Daniel's future hunting companion and friend, wrote that "[Sarah] loved Daniel above all her children" and their bond was powerful and affectionate.[62] Although Daniel was often wayward and unruly, Sarah praised his independence, perhaps more than a mother should have. Perhaps from the beginning, she understood that Daniel's curiosity was driven by a peculiar fervor for the ancient and wild crags and mists beyond the family farm.

---

[59] Draper, Lyman C. *The Life of Daniel Boone.* Ted Franklin Belue, ed. Mechanicsburg: Stackpole Books, 1998. 111.
[60] Draper, Lyman C. *The Life of Daniel Boone,* 6.
[61] Boone, *My Father, Daniel Boone.* 10
[62] Houston, Peter. *A Sketch of the Life and Character of Daniel Boone.* Ted Franklin Belue, ed. Mechanicsburg: Stackple Books, 1997. 12.

A Curiously Restless Youth

It is believed that Daniel authored two autobiographies. After more than five years of intense study and historical analysis, however, it seems clear that, while it comforts us to think that this representative American man and overall badass of Western history cared as much about his legacy as us moderns do, he failed to protect it from the many rivers, fires, and battles his journey crossed, experienced, and fought. On my library's shelf, there is a title that stares at me with his name in the place of the author's, although the words contained between its covers are only distant representations of *his* truth.

It begins with a phrase that, while not altogether his in original genius, describes what I believe is an accurate description of the man of Daniel Boone. "Curiosity is natural to the soul of man."[63] With these simple words begin both an epic and treatise—a story rich with adventure and a thesis intent on instructing humankind. Perhaps by design, it reminds the reader of the first words of Book 1 Sections 1 and 2 of Aristotle's *Politics,* wherein Aristotle declares, "Every state is a community" and that man, the chief of the community, "is more of a political animal" than his animal neighbors. These words, taken perhaps out of their context and placed coarsely into ours, paint man, nature, and communities as distinct entities that both share and do not share certain qualities. Man is political and man is curious. Perhaps that is the same thing. But, as Aristotle claims, man's curiosity apart from "law and justice" make him little better than the worst of the animals.

---

[63] Boone, Daniel. *The Adventures of Colonel Daniel Boone, Formerly a Hunter; Containing a Narrative of the Wars of Kentucky, as Given by Himself.* 1.

Regardless of the fabricated author or Aristotle's musings, Daniel Boone was curious, and his youth knew little moderation. As long as a frontier existed to be explored, Daniel was determined to be its chief explorer. If his father provided his itching foot and wanderlust, his mother provided his fervor for the frontier. With such a velocity, his position was clear: forever onward into new directions and uncharted frontiers. This evident yet enigmatic curiosity was visible from the beginning. Daniel's drive to know the unknown sometimes surpassed his concern for how others might worry about his extended absences, for his adoration for the woods, his curiosity, and his general restlessness trumped all else. As I said, little moderation.

The woods of the early Pennsylvania frontier teemed with life—deer, bear, buffalo, wild turkeys, and small game. It is believed that the nearby "Flying Hill" was so titled from the "perpetual flutter of wild turkeys there."[64] Daniel was enchanted. As a youth, he was "delighted to range in the woods, watch the wild animals, and contemplate the beauties of uncultivated nature," wrote one early twentieth-century historian.[65] Between the ages of ten and seventeen, Daniel acted as the family herdsman. Cowboys of the early American West bear little resemblance to the Western cowboys made popular in the mid-twentieth century by Hollywood movies and characters such as John Wayne. Push past the exciting cattle drives, clever lasso throws, chaps, spurs, and big hats—herdsmanship of this period more closely resembled meditation than farming. In the morning, Daniel was responsible for walking the herd out to the

---

[64] Bakeless, *Daniel Boone.* 7.
[65] Peck, John Mason. "Life of Daniel Boone, The Pioneer of Kentucky" in *Makers of American History.* New York: The University Society, 1904. 4.

pasture, the area the cattle were to graze that day. All day, he would make sure they ate, a thing most cows do without any stimulation. With the setting sun, Daniel was responsible to then bring the cows back to the yard, for protection and shelter. Enthralled yet? Daniel wasn't either.

Pastoral life made him accustomed to being near the woods, and he would often carry a club—"a grub dug up by the roots, nicely shaven down, leaving a rooty knob at the end, which he called his 'herdsman club.'" Along with the cattle, he would bring home many a dead bird or small game to the un-wanting family table.[66] Silently creeping amidst the woods, he would toss his club at birds and small pray. With only observation and experience as his guide, he quickly became an apt scholar on "the peculiar habits of birds and wild animals," writes a primary Boone historian, Lyman Draper.[67] Later, after his father bought him a "short-barreled rifle," probably a large-caliber European fowling piece, he became an adept marksman and harvested more substantial game.[68] Technology in the hands of an artist is beauty.

Watch the cows? He was in the woods. Abandoning the business of herding, Daniel ventured far into the Flying Hills, Oley Hills, and Neversink Mountains—a modern day Nature Preserve and hiking trail—for extended winter hunts by the age of thirteen. Writing of such a time, Nathan Boone later remarked, "My father…would go hunting at the slightest opportunity," or no opportunity at all.[69] Although he tried his hand at the family farm, blacksmith shop, and mill, Daniel "never took any delight in farming or stock raising" and was

---

[66] Boone, *My Father, Daniel Boone.* 11.
[67] Draper, *The Life of Daniel Boone.* 111.
[68] Lofaro, *Daniel Boone.* 4.
[69] Lofaro, *Daniel Boone.* 11-13.

"ever unpracticed in the business of farming," wrote Daniel's nephew, Daniel Boone Bryan.[70] Rather, Daniel always gravitated towards the woods. It was where his love for the chase deepened into a life-long passion, where his iron steadiness with a rifle and animal-like ability to subsist in nature developed and deepened. It was his frontier; it was his home.

During these forays, Daniel's curiosity found its way into even deeper mischief. Daniel befriended his father's blacksmith, Henry Miller, although he was two or three years his senior. Lyman Draper described Daniel's crony as

> raised on the outskirts of civilization, fearless of self-denials and hardship. Under an exterior somewhat rough was concealed a heart faithful in its friendships and generous in its impulses.[71]

They found in one another congenial and lively spirits of mischief and amusement.

As one story goes, George Wilcoxen, a local man entirely inept and untrained in the practical uses of the musket, desired to try his hand at deer hunting. Needing to acquire a weapon, Wilcoxen borrowed Squire Boone's and requested that he load the firearm the night before so it would be prepared for "early morning use." During the night, Daniel and Henry unloaded the musket's contents and added "half a dozen" times the usual load of powder, balls, and shot.[72] At the "peep of day,"

---

[70] Daniel Boone Bryan to Draper, Feb. 27, 1843, Draper Manuscripts 22C5; Faragher, John Mack. *Daniel Boone: the Life and Legend of an American Pioneer*. New York: Henry Hold and Company, 1992. 31.

[71] Draper, *The Life of Daniel Boone*. 113.

[72] Boone, *My Father, Daniel Boone*. 12; Morgan, *Boone: A Biography*. 14; Draper, *The Life of Daniel Boone*. 113.

34

however, and as Wilcoxen took the musket into the nearby forest, both boys had misgivings about their deed.[73] They feared that, by overloading the musket, it would burst upon firing, killing or seriously wounding the naïve and unsuspecting hunter. But it was too late.

Following the sunrise, the entire town's slumber was interrupted by the report of a canon in its wooded periphery. Running to the scene of the crime, Daniel and Henry discovered the triumphant hunter alive and smiling. The explosion had knocked Wilcoxen over with only temporary—nonetheless bloody—injuries on his nose and forehead. In his 1851 interview, Nathan Boone described such wounds as a "gash in his forehead down to the skull…and badly bruised."[74] Although Wilcoxen claimed to have shot a deer in the process, it is unclear whether his prize was ever discovered. Regardless, Daniel's mischief had found a relief and the naïve hunter bragging rights.

Daniel's mischief was also restless. During the widespread smallpox epidemic of 1738-39, his mother confined him and his siblings at home to prevent their exposure to the disease. Four years old, Daniel found the solitary confinement of the Boone homestead irksome and he itched for freedom. Beyond his years, Daniel saw a solution: if he could take the disease, his mother would be forced to forgo his incarceration and allow him to wander without worry. After the rest of the house went to bed, Daniel and his older sister Elizabeth slipped out to the neighbor's house and crept into bed with the smallpox patient. "Cheerfully anticipating the worse," they awaited the sign of their freedom.[75]

---

[73] Draper, *The Life of Daniel Boone.* 113.
[74] Boone, *My Father, Daniel Boone.* 13.
[75] Bakeless, *Daniel Boone.* 14.

It soon took. After Daniel confessed to the obvious truth with "childlike simplicity and without the least reserve," Sarah Boone scolded him: "Thee naughty little gorrel, why did thee not tell me before so that I could have had thee better prepared?"[76] Sarah's response is truly revealing—perhaps even more so than Daniel's actions. Her words are devoid of genuine surprise. She called him a "gorrel," the old English equivalent of "lout," and blames him not for the act, but his naivety for not warning her beforehand. She did not question his nature, just the lack of its warning. Sarah Boone seemed to exemplify Alexis de Tocqueville's maxim: "The man is so to speak a whole in the swaddling clothes of his cradle."[77]

A Natural Education

As for Daniel's education, little is known and much is "disputed."[78] In 1748, the German Reverend Henry Melchoir Muhlenberg critiqued Oley's school, writing, "In Oley sind die Schulen sehr entfernt."[79] It appears that these "sehr entfernt" (very isolated) schools were a part of the Lutheran church, making it hard—on both accounts—for a Quaker child living on the frontier to attend. Later in life, Daniel was in the habit of telling his children that he never attended any formal schooling. With "his hand writing…a scrawl," Daniel's "spelling always had a wild, free, original flavor, like his life," writes historian

---

[76] Draper, *The Life of Daniel Boone.* 110.
[77] Alexis de Tocqueville. *Democracy in America.* trans., ed., Harvey C. Mansfield. Chicago: The University of Chicago Press, 2000. 28.
[78] Lofaro, *Daniel Boone.* 4.
[79] Roughly translated, "In Oley, the schools are very distant." Quote taken from *The Governor's Messages and Reports of the Heads of Departments of the Commonwealth of Pennsylvania*, Part II. 1877.

John Bakeless.[80] It appears the entirety of our young hunter's education was at home—or in the woods.

In his father's hearth and shop he learned a practical knowledge. Although the particulars of his book learning remain unclear, according to legend, Daniel's uncle John Boone attempted to school him in the ways of the letter. Daniel's flawed orthography, however, quickly frustrated his teacher, wherein Squire responded, "Let the girls do the spelling and Dan will do the shooting."[81] Although his letters, orders, survey books, and accounts display "creative spelling" and an education never perfected, Daniel's children and grandchildren later remarked that he was a lifelong lover of reading and, although his letters were rough, their rhythm and lyric were eloquent.[82]

In the woods, Daniel learned a natural knowledge, based upon the sweeping and open halls of nature. He quickly became an adept scholar of the lingua franca of the forest, as his "strength of mind, keen habits of observation, and imperturbable tranquility under…perils" were the fundamental building blocks for his unrivaled success under these natural and feral volumes. Late-nineteenth-century historian John S. C. Abbott writes of such perfection

> No marksman could surpass him in the dexterity with which his bullet he would strike the head of a nail, at the distance of many yards. No Indian hunter or warrior could with more sagacity trace his steps through the pathless

---

[80] Bakeless, *Daniel Boone.* 10.

[81] Bakeless, *Daniel Boone.* 11.

[82] It is generally accepted that his favorite books, which he had on him always, was the Bible and Gulliver's Travels. Source: Morgan, *Boone: A Biography.* xii.

forest, detect the footsteps of a retreating foe, or search out the hiding place of the panther or the bear.[83]

Observing the lessons of the snow and the leaf, of the moss and the track, and of the movement and the prowess of the Indian warrior, and experiencing the wonders and complexities of the forest's ebbs and flows, of the stars awakening in reverence, and of the flowers, animals, and mountains' reflected wisdom, Daniel's scholarship under the tutelage of the forest was refined at an early age.[84]

According to Xenophon, the Greek historian, soldier, philosopher, and contemporary of Socrates, Daniel had the very best of educations. Believing that the "first efforts of a youth emerging from boyhood should be directed to the institution of the chase," he offered his own advice for the rearing and education of boys

> My advice to the young is, do not despise hunting or the other training of your boyhood, if you desire to grow up to be good men, good not only in war but in all else of which the issue is perfection in thought, word, and deed.[85]

Xenophon equated him who is educated by the hunt as both "the true noble" and civilization's "saviour." He believed that the education of the hunt provides most all that is needed to become a man, for it molds a "sound soul" that is trained and readied for the "real world of actual things;" it deprives youths of "evil

---

[83] Abbott, John S. *Daniel Boone: The Pioneer of Kentucky.* New York: Dodd, Mead & Company, 1874. 42-43.

[84] This last part is taken from Ralph Waldo Emerson's essay on Nature, Chapter 1.

[85] Xenophon, "On Hunting" in *Selections.* H. G. Dakyns. 224-225.

pleasures," which ought "never to be learned;" and it instills in the hunter "a passion for manly virtue." It is through such an education that justice becomes "familiar to tongue and ear" and nobility can manifest in both private and public society.[86]

Although Daniel's early life was "unpracticed" in farming, mischievous in nature, and governed by supreme wanderlust, his character was forever impressed by such an adventurous and curious youth, for it was reared in an atmosphere of freedom, illimitable forests, and the hunt.

---

[86] Xenophon, *Selections*. 274-275.

CHAPTER 3

The Warrior's Trace

The Pisgah Vision

There it was—the Promised Land. Standing atop Pilot Knob in June 1769, the thirty-four-year-old woodsman beheld miles of fabled forests cloaked in a distant blue haze and fused with sensuous and seemingly untouched gardens. It was Daniel Boone's first glimpse of the Great Meadow, the epic Bluegrass Island. It was a land "well calculated to impress the beholder with a reverential sense of the stupendous works of the Almighty Architect."[87] It was a vision of Eden; it was a hunter's paradise; it was *Kanta-ke*. Writing of this moment, Daniel remembered

> Just at the close of day the gentle gales retired, and left the place to the disposal of a profound calm. Not a breeze shook the most tremulous leaf. I had gained the summit of a commanding ridge, and, looking round with astonishing delight, beheld the ample plains, the beauteous tracts below. On the other hand, I surveyed the famous river Ohio that rolled in silent dignity, marking the western

---

[87] Draper, *The Life of Daniel Boone.* 177.

boundary of Kentucke with inconceivable grandeur. At a vast distance I beheld the mountains lift their venerable brows, and penetrate the clouds. All things were still.

Such a calm and still moment was Daniel's Pisgah vision— Pisgah was the biblical mountain in which Moses ascended to view the Land of Canaan after years of wandering in the wilderness. Unlike Moses, however, Daniel's destiny lay in front of him.

In such a "pure white moment," to quote Mary Oliver's poem, *Such Singing in the Wild Branches,* Daniel remembered, "No populous city, with all the varieties of commerce and stately structures, could afford so much pleasure to my mind, as the beauties of nature I found here." It was a land of promise— of milk and honey—and of supreme beauty. Like Moses, however, Daniel first had to wander.

The Yadkin

If Daniel's early youth forever impressed his character, his family's move to North Carolina's Yadkin Valley in 1750 entirely captivated his mind's curiosity and gave a supreme outlet to his soul's restlessness. The mid-eighteenth century saw a steady stream of settlers migrating to the rich and now pricy lands of the Pennsylvanian frontier. It was a land steadily bled, cleared, and plowed by the first pioneer families. It was now ripe for the homesteading farmer.

Once a hunter's paradise, Daniel's woods became populated and the game of its near periphery receded deeper into the woods. Squire Boone and his family found the growing countryside of Berks County unpleasant and disagreeable as early as 1748. Maybe, perhaps, "something called...something beyond the mountains...whispered."[88] Lyman Draper writes

> "The choice lands of the settlement were all located, and as more homesteads were needed, it became a matter of much concern and inquiry to what new, fertile, and salubrious country they could migrate where the right to the soil could be cheaply purchased."[89]

Procuring new land for cheap was an electrifying proposal. America was, in one (small) sense, a land for the taking. It did not require a title, a name, or wealth. Instead, capturing the American opportunity required a steadfast mind, hardy family, and, most importantly, an iron soul. Maybe, perhaps, it required an American soul. Underneath this opportunity rested the ancient and prominently European myth of a new Eden, discovered beyond the sea or the mountains. The call of the American West was, for some, a search for this New Eden. For others, it was for new beginnings. For the Boones however, it was a place to spread out—a place to satisfy their curiosity and house their wanderlust.

By 1749, Squire's family had increased to eleven children and his once "gently rolling countryside" undulated with neighbors. Additionally, the farming of those days exhausted the soil. Early eighteenth century frontier agriculture was based solely on conquering a wild land to produce enough of a yield to feed your family today, tomorrow, and through the harsh winter. Why should they have done any different? There

---

[88] Bakeless, *Daniel Boone.* 5.
[89] Draper, *The Life of Daniel Boone.* 124.

was always more soil one step to the west. The mathematics of frontier farming was simple. If you did not produce enough food and fuel, your family would starve and freeze. It was a simple life, but a really hard life. One had to fight not only the restraining and arduous geographic elements of the untamed frontier but the climate and cultures within such elements as well.

It appears that during the early spring of 1749, already pestered by growing populations at home, Squire would have seen dozens of settler families passing through to the deeper frontier of the Shenandoah River and its great interior valley. Squire's familial need and "itching foot" was spurred on by the reports brought back by adventurous pioneers of the "fertility and beauty of those solitudes, where conscience was free, labor voluntary, and a comfortable living easily obtained."[90] Important for Daniel, however, such pioneers were also cloaked in their great success on the hunt.

Already, Joseph Stover, Daniel's uncle, had emigrated to the headwaters of the South Fork of the Shenandoah River. It was with Joseph that Squire had immigrated to the New World forty years before, and, perhaps, it was because of Joseph's success within the great interior valley that Squire finally chose to move his family into the deeper frontier. The decision appears to have been made immediately, during the winter of 1749-50. In the January 1750 Minutes of the Woman's Meeting of the Exeter Quakers, Sarah Boone is recorded to have requested a letter of transfer "to Friends in Virginia, Carolina or elsewhere."[91] On April 11, Squire sold his Exeter homestead to

---

[90] Draper, *The Life of Daniel Boone.* 124.
[91] Faragher, *Daniel Boone.* 26.

his cousin, William Mogridge, for £300, or nearly $86,000 today.[92] Spring had dawned and the Boones had gone.

The snows had melted and their white blanket vanished but there were no cattle in Boone's fields, no fiber in his mill, and no fire in his shop. The raucous ping of molten metal had subsided, for the founding family of Exeter Township was once again on the move to new frontiers. With their "small drove of cattle," the Boone family departed the Pennsylvanian countryside on May 1st for the fertile and open lands of the southwest.[93] Their destination: the new frontier.

Sure of only their direction, the Boone family packed into three or four Conestoga wagons. Distinctive in shape and size, large teams of five or more horses were required to drive these large vessels. They were built with the West in mind: their haul was uniquely designed with curved floors to prevent shifting or bending over the rough terrain; sturdy and waterproof white canvas stretched across their wooden frames to protect against inclement weather; their carrying capacity of nearly twelve thousand pounds accommodated large families and their goods. Most importantly, however, the Conestoga design was heavy, even freight-like, and capable of traversing long distances—and of transporting the East to the West.

It is believed that the party included Squire's nine unmarried children, ranging from three to nineteen years of age: two married sons and daughters-in-law, his married daughter with her husband and baby, and perhaps some extended family as well. Regardless of the particulars, the Boones always traveled in family units. Squire, the patriarch, led the party of eighteen or more, and Daniel, the sixteen-year-old

---

[92] Bakeless, *Daniel Boone.* 18.
[93] Bakeless, *Daniel Boone,* 18.

accomplished woodsman, guided its path. With his gun on his shoulder and his eye due southwest, Daniel's job was to scout for the trail, game, and any potential harm lurking in the near periphery of the wagon train.

It was customary for the women to ride in the wagons while the men fought the trail in the front and drove the cattle in the rear. In this case, however, Daniel was positioned in front of the line. Perhaps Squire knew that, if trusted with the cattle, Daniel would become lost in the chase and forget about his duties. Like his uncle, Daniel Morgan, a woodsman and the future General and hero of the American Revolution, Daniel now led his family into the mysterious country of the American Southwest. The Boones' wanderlust—their itching foot—was quelled, if only for the moment.

Daniel's internal compass always pointed due west. After crossing the Schuylkill and taking Harris's Ferry across the Susquehanna, the Boones bid adieu to Pennsylvania. Traversing through the Maryland countryside and crossing the Potomac at Williamsport, the Boone family entered the great valley of Virginia. Their path is known today as the Allegheny Trail. Traveling fifteen miles a day, Daniel's role as guide was crucial: the wagons needed cleared and dry trails and their living cargo required sustenance.

Although their approximate route can today be traced by U.S. highways, at the time, it put Daniel's deep knowledge of the woods and navigation to the test. Curving with the Appalachian Mountains, Daniel navigated through the principal artery connecting the Native peoples of the North to those of the South. Employing his experience with Indian traces and his understanding of centuries-old Indian communication customs, he guided his family safely through the "Virginian Road," now U.S. 11, and fed them well along the way.

The party appears to have tarried for two years on Linville Creek in Virginia, claimed Daniel's youngest son, Nathan Boone.[94] Linville Creek's name originated from one of its earliest residents, who is believed to have been "slain by Indians in the mountain region above the head of the Yadkin."[95] It was also the home of Squire's old friend John Lincoln. In 1779, Daniel would return to Linville Creek to personally lead John's son, Abraham Lincoln, through the Cumberland Gap and into Kentucky, where he would construct a small but historic log cabin. Without an adept and skilled woodsman as their guide, who knows if Lincoln's journey into the wilderness would have ultimately changed the course of history?

The Boones' camp was a few miles from modern-day Harrisonburg, Rockingham County, Virginia, and it remained there for one to two growing seasons. This pause, however, irked Daniel's restless soul. It was during this time in 1750 that Daniel's love for the long hunt began. While his family remained to farm, Daniel bent to the patterns of his youth amidst woodland Indian cultures and began increasingly extended forays into the wilderness for fur, wild game and, most importantly, adventure. Daniel, accompanied by his childhood comrade Henry Miller, left the banks of Linville Creek and traveled past the Shenandoah Mountains and down the Roanoke River near Big Lick, which later became Roanoke, Virginia.

Their hunt took them deeper southwest then either of the young hunters had ever been. From Big Lick, they followed the eastern path through the Roanoke Gap, traveling through the

---

[94] Boone, *My Father, Daniel Boone.* 12.
[95] Draper, *The Life of Daniel Boone.* 125.

Blue Ridge and then south into the great Piedmont country. Through the rich canebrakes, the young hunters tracked bear, elk, deer, panthers, wildcats, and wolves. Perhaps even buffalo. After a fruitful summer and early fall, the hunters took their harvest of hides north to Philadelphia, reaping substantial gain from its ill-supplied markets.

Henry Miller later remembered this extended hunting expedition as the great turning point of his life. Both Daniel and Henry had tasted the sublimity of the West and had reaped its bountiful harvest, yet the frontier's peculiar power operated quite differently on the two souls. They were both at the age when young men catch sight of their own paths and begin to see their destiny. Although they were great friends and woodsmen, their 1750 extended frolic in the wilderness revealed divergent paths. While Henry would become a substantial landholder and establish a notable and highly profitable ironworks in Augusta County, Virginia, Daniel's journey was forever westward. While the experience fostered the desire for home in the first, it fermented wanderlust for the frontier in the other. If the horizon's providential call had thus far been unclear to Daniel, its glorious rays were now slowly rising above the western mountains.

Daniel was not alone in his wanderlust, however. While he was away on his long hunt, land records reveal that Squire Boone's restless spirit was also irked by the family's pause. During the fall of 1750, Squire ventured ahead of his family to North Carolina for land speculation. By October, he had filed a warrant claiming six hundred and forty acres near the banks of the Yadkin River near Grants Creek. One historian remembered the Yadkin as a "clear, rapid-flowing mountain stream, offering excellent opportunities for mill sites."[96] It was a land "punctuated by beautiful meadows, perfect for grazing livestock, and well-watered lowlands where the soil was fertile clay, brick-red when plowed and exposed to the sun."[97]

The Forks of the Yadkin bore striking contrast to the black soil Squire was accustomed to in Pennsylvania. He had selected the site himself, amongst the thousands of square miles up for the taking by the Earl of Granville—who owned a great majority of the northern quadrant of the colony. It was a wilder and more diverse land than Pennsylvania. The Yadkin River Valley was the extreme western frontier of Anglo settlement. Squire's choice land ultimately boasted a scenic overlook of the Yadkin River in what was then Rowan County—today Davidson County, North Carolina.[98] Upon this hill he would build the first family cabin. Squire had found his home.

After Daniel returned from the North and Squire from the South, the Boone family reanimated their wagons once again. From Linville Creek, the family traveled directly to Squire's land on the Forks, a near-three-hundred-mile journey. Records are sparse, but the family must have settled on the land by late 1751. Rumor suggests that, because they reached the land late in the year, the family spent their first North Carolinian winter in a cave near the river—known today as "Boone's Cave." More likely, however, Squire established a cabin on his mount by late 1751 with the help of his sons. In either case, the Boones' presence was felt in February of the following year when a neighboring plot of land was described as oriented "on the E. side of the path that leads from Sandy Creek Ford to

[96] Faragher, *Daniel Boone.* 29.
[97] Faragher, *Daniel Boone.* 29.
[98] Bakeless, *Daniel Boone.* 19.

Squire Boon's."[99] Lyman Draper's notes also record that, by autumn of 1752, Squire's daughter Elizabeth was wedded in the Yadkin Valley to one William Grant, "a native of Maryland who had been some years residing in that region."[100]

By 1753, Squire had purchased two additional six-hundred-and-forty-acre tracts of land for his growing family, near modern-day Mocksville, North Carolina.[101] Although the location of the Boone homestead changed and its landholdings increased immensely, "the Boones transplanted to the Yadkin a landscape of kinship very similar to the one they had left behind in Pennsylvania."[102] They may have been travelers, but they always traveled together.

Nature's Call

In 1700, the English explorer, ecologist, and writer John Lawson observed that the Yadkin Valley was

> very good and free from Grubs and Underwood. A man near Sapona [the Yadkin] may more easily clear ten Acres of Ground than in some places he can one…That day we passed through a delicious Country (none that I ever saw exceeds it.) We saw fine bladed grass six feet high, along the Banks of these pleasant Rivulets.[103]

---

[99] Faragher, *Daniel Boone.* 30.
[100] Draper, *The Life of Daniel Boone.* 125.
[101] Brown, Meredith Mason. *Frontiersman: Daniel Boone and the Making of America.* Baton Rouge: Louisiana State University Press, 2008. 10.
[102] Faragher, *Daniel Boone.* 30.
[103] Lawson, John. *History of North Carolina.* Charlotte: Observer Printing House, 1903.

As "giant sycamores and tulip poplars, eight, ten, or sometimes fourteen feet in diameter" capped the valley's bottomlands, the chief labor of its settlers lay in the clearing of fields—a task achieved by girdling. It was a grueling but effective process of frontier settlement. By "hacking rings" around the tree's entire circumference, the tree would slowly choke, as the "lifeblood of sap in the bark from root to branch tips" was cut off.[104] Thus strangled, the commanding tree would slowly rot, dropping meager branches the first year and large limbs the second. Girdled trees would inevitably fall, leaving the remaining fields open for the plow. It was a long and drawn out process—a process that Daniel could live without.

However, Jethro Rumple, another early settler, wrote that the Yadkin region overall was "destitute of forest," for large numbers of buffalo had created over the centuries a veldt-like landscape of lightly shaded prairies and fertile plains. Rumple observed that "wild deer mingled with the horses and cattle as they grazed."[105] In addition to the supporting wildlife, the Yadkin's ecology also contained myriads of rivulets that combined into larger steams and ultimately flowed into the Catawba and Yadkin rivers. It was a bisected, fertile, and well-watered landscape where game was abundant and food aplenty.

In the spring of 1751, the Boone family set out to clear their new homestead. Such a task is somewhat unimaginable for modern man. To open a land that had continual grass or tree or shrub cover for thousands of years was no small task, and there were no chainsaws. The forest of the river valley was dense and

---

[104] Morgan, *Boone: A Biography*. 34.
[105] *A History of Rowan County, North Carolina, Containing Sketches of Prominent Families and Distinguished Men* (Salisbury, N.C.: J. J. Bruner, 1881), 28.

its roots were deep. It was an old land with old stories, comparable perhaps to J. R. R. Tolkien's mythical Fangorn Forest. Speaking of such age, Treebeard, Tolkien's elder tree, declared

> 'I am not going to tell you my name, not yet at any rate.' A queer half-knowing, half-humorous look came with a green flicker into his eyes. 'For one thing it would take a long while: my name is growing all the time, and I've lived a very long, long time; so my name is like a story. Real names tell you the story of things they belong to in my language, in the Old Entish as you might say. It is a lovely language, but it takes a very long time saying anything in it, because we do not say anything in it, unless it is worth taking a long time to say, and to listen to.'

Daniel's spirit longed for the living woods and the vitality of the hunt—not for the rotting wooded corpses of his father's fields. Daniel hungered to hear the "lovely language" of the wood's real name.

Puhpohwee. The language of the Potawatomi—a nation of the indigenous peoples of the Great Plains and Great Lakes regions—is called *Bodewadmimwen,* a dialect of Algonquian. A language similar to Old Entish, *Bodewadmimwen* is an old yet living language that recognizes not the male and female within its nouns and verbs but the animate and inanimate. Out of this "grammar of animacy," writes Robin Wall Kimmerer, communication becomes community and language takes on a power of its own. Trees become someones, not somethings, and the damp woods become a home, not a place. To speak of life, the verb, "to be," the Potawatomi say *Yawe*. "Isn't it just what it means, to be, to have the breath of life within, to be the offspring of creation?" writes Kimmerer.

Puhpowhee roughly translates as "the force which causes [life] to push up from the earth overnight." It is the unseen energy that animates, propels, and connects; it is a story that grows; and it is our story. One could imagine that the majority of Daniel's prayers were pleas for rain. Not in the same custom and rhythm of a farmer's prayer, but in an earnest desire to capture the rain's precious gift: an afternoon away from the plow and in the woods. Perhaps Daniel was the sort who felt the forest's beating heart during the rain, as the damp air invigorates the forest's rich successions and wonders—*Puhpowhee*. Perhaps Daniel felt a homely solitude in the woods, a peace that his thoughts were safe within its wooded and damp succulence. Alone is a word without meaning in the forest.

It was during Daniel's early years on the Yadkin that his reputation as a notable trapper, guide, and woodsman flourished. By his late teens, Daniel was widely known and highly regarded amongst Yadkin hunters. Although Penn's woods provided him with ample room for adventure, the Yadkin was a truly wild place. It was a world similar to what his father experienced in early Pennsylvania over thirty years prior—a world with little Anglo contact and a world entirely uncharted and rough; it was world similar to his mother's Welsh homeland; and it was a new start with infinite possibilities. The virgin periphery of the setting sun had always drawn Daniel towards its fleeting rays. Now, however, he was closer to it than ever.

It is important to note that, although "The West" is most often categorized by the gunslinger cowboys of the latter half of the nineteenth century, the true frontier saga of the American West began centuries earlier and on the eastern side of the Appalachians. While the cattle drivers, cowboys, and prairie Indians present a highly romantic epic of lead and powder—of engine and rail—it was the early "pedestrian sod-busters who tamed the bulk of the West."[106] The initial pioneers sought freedom by land and desired the equality and life only the frontier could offer. By the late-seventeenth century, the British colonial arm stretched the breadth of the Atlantic seaboard from modern day New Hampshire to Georgia. This coastal belt quickly became overcrowded and the colonists needed more land. Territorial expansion could proceed in only one direction—west. West into the uncharted primordial wilderness beyond the wooded periphery and into the shadows of the Appalachian Mountains.

In his book, *The Mammoth Book of the West,* Jon E. Lewis painted the early West as

> The unknown and magic forest land which lay beyond the cultivated fields of the tidewater colonialists and stretched away to the forbidding ridges of the Appalachians, which walled the coastal plain.[107]

Under these magical and "forbidden ridges" Daniel's frontier saga began. One could imagine him perched on his father's scenic overlook, leaning on his rifle with his eyes fixed on the setting sun, every moment his soul growing disproportionally to the sun's sublime retreat beyond the wooded canopy. From his

---

[106] Lewis, Jon E. *The Mammoth Book of The West: The Making of the American West.* New York: Carroll & Graf Publishers, Inc., 1996. (xii).
[107] Lewis, *The Mammoth Book of The West.* 10.

cabin door, the distant and majestic ridges of the Alleghany Mountains, "rising six thousand feet into the clouds," pierced his soul and tempted his dreams.[108]

Early Boone historian John Bakeless noted that "no roads ran that way except the 'Warriors' Path,' a mere 'trace' used only by red hunters or war parties."[109] Such a path, if it could be found, would lead through the *Ouasioto*, or Cumberland, Mountains and into the deep west of its inner valleys.[110] *Ouasioto* was either a Wyandotte or Shawnee word: *scioto,* meaning "Deer's Path."[111] In his *Indian Trails of the Southeast,* historian William E. Myer wrote that the Warriors' Path was "almost invisible, save to the practiced eye of the Indian." The Appalachians stood as a tangled and wooded blockade, concealing the mysterious path West. For now, Daniel's eyes alone were able to follow the sun, for no white man knew the way the path twisted, turned, and ultimately vanished through the mountains. Years passed.

Meeting of Woodsmen

"Fate came plodding down the Yadkin Valley Road one day, leading a pack-horse," wrote John Bakeless.[112] For the moment, such fortune was personified as a backwoods and itinerant Irish peddler. His name was John Findley (some

---

[108] Abbott, John S. *Daniel Boone: The Pioneer of Kentucky.* New York: Dodd, Mead & Company, 1874. 51.
[109] Bakeless, *Daniel Boone.* 15.
[110] Draper, *The Life of Daniel Boone.* 207.
[111] Harrison, Lowell H., Dawson Nelson L. *A Kentucky Sampler: Essays from The Filson Club History Quarterly 1926—1976.* University Press of Kentucky, 1977. 16.
[112] Bakeless, *Daniel Boone.* 44.

historians spell his name John Finely). It had been fourteen years since their paths crossed on Braddock's 1755 campaign, where Findley filled fireside tales with accounts of a great meadowland beyond the mountains.[113] He described a land of "cane and clover," of "fertile valleys," and "wild game…beyond [imagination]." Beyond the sublime and Edenic romance, however, Findley also spoke of "great profits for hunters, trappers, and traders."[114]

He had recently returned from a fur trading expedition with the Shawnee at Blue Licks Town, or *Skipaki-thiki*. The name *Skipaki*, is Shawnee for "blue" and *thiki* means "place."[115] However, the Iroquois Confederacy referred to such a region as *Kanta-ke,* an Iroquois word meaning meadows or fields. While there is much disagreement and debate over the lexical origins of the name *Kentucky*, it would appear that Americans favored the Iroquois place name—*Kanta-ke*—over that of the Shawnees—*Skipaki-thiki*.

Although the great and vast expanse of the American frontier tended to engulf and even scatter men, fate seemed to blow John Findley directly to the doorstep of Daniel Boone's log cabin in 1768 or 1769. "[Findley] was just one more of those itinerant merchants who wandered with their moveable stores among the backwoods settlements," remembered one historian.[116] Findley's fortuitous stop at Daniel's hearth, however, would provide a unique and exceptionally promising reward for both. Many years later, Nathan Boone remembered

---

[113] Boone, *My Father, Daniel Boone.* 17.
[114] Faragher, *Daniel Boone.* 70.
[115] Hanna, Charles A. *The Wilderness Trail: The Ventures and Adventurers of the Pennsylvania Traders on the Allegheny Path.* New York: The Knickerbocker Press, 1911. 256.
[116] Bakeless, *Daniel Boone.* 44.

that, after stabling his "spare nags," Findley and his father spent hours in front of the warm fire talking of "Kaintuck." A year earlier in 1767, Daniel had attempted and failed to reach Kentucky by route of the Big Sandy River. Findley believed that the Cherokee Indians frequented a warpath—a meager trace— that crossed the mountains.[117]

While spindling his yarn beside Daniel's fire, Findley rehearsed his 1752 trip down the Ohio in a canoe.[118] After landing on Kentucky's shore near the mouth of Big Bone Creek, he met a company of Shawnee headed into the interior of Kentucky. Findley was "invited" to attend their expedition. Readily assenting and fearing for his life, his travels ultimately landed him at an Indian settlement near Lulbegrud Creek of the northern tributary of the Red River in Kentucky.[119] Lyman Draper noted the Indian settlement was "directly on the route of the great *Warriors' Road* leading from the Ohio southward through the Cumberland Gap."[120] It also appears to be the settlement that Benjamin Franklin referenced when he claimed, "in the year 1752, the Six Nations, Shawanesse and Delawares had a large town on the Kentucke River."[121] What Findley witnessed during this expedition could only be compared with the perfections and supreme bounty of Genesis' Eden

[Buffalo] herds so huge that a man had to be careful lest he be crushed to death in their mad stampedes. The ground

---

[117] Boone, *My Father, Daniel Boone.* 23.

[118] Draper, *The Life of Daniel Boone.* 205.

[119] Lyman Draper noted in his history of Daniel Boone that the name of Lulbegrud was given to the stream by a party of early explorers encamped on its banks, who happened to have a copy of *Gulliver's Travels* with them, from which they derived the unpleasing appellation.

[120] Draper, *The Life of Daniel Boone.* 205.

[121] Franklin, Benjamin. *Ohio Settlement*, London, 1772, p. 44.

rumbling with their hoofs. At the Falls of the Ohio, wild geese and ducks so plentiful there was no need even to kill them. All a man could eat were drawn by the current over the falls and thrown up freshly killed on the banks below. One might pick up enough fresh fowl for dinner any day. And land—land such as a man might dream of. Well watered, lush and green, with fertile soil in all directions. Endless acres for the taking. A settler's paradise. A hunter's paradise, too, with deerskins at a dollar each.[122]

Findley's "enthusiastic love of nature" betrayed, perhaps, his descriptions of Kentucky as the land of plenty as described in the Bible.[123] His stories, however tainted, found in Daniel an ardent and devoted audience. Fellow hunter and personal friend Peter Houston wrote in his 1842 *Sketch of the Life and Character of Daniel Boone,* "[Findley's] description enthused Daniel, who never rested until" his soul beheld the great meadow beyond the horizon. Draper went so far to note that Findley's recital revived Daniel's soul, writing that it sparked "feelings of peculiar delight" in his bosom.[124]

Findley and Daniel both attempted to cross into the Promised Land via mountain pass. Both had failed in their own way. Although an adept trader and hunter, able to navigate the Ohio with ease, Findley was somewhat disoriented on land. His trading relations with the Cherokee had taught him that many Indian and buffalo traces connected the coastal lands of the East to the inner valleys of the West, but his insufficient skills as a woodsman prevented him from finding them.

---

[122] Bakeless, *Daniel Boone.* 45.
[123] Draper, *The Life of Daniel Boone.* 207.
[124] Draper, *The Life of Daniel Boone.* 207.

Daniel, on the other hand, lacked both the knowledge of such traces and an understanding of what the great meadow— *Kanta-ke*—of Kentucky looked like. This may seem obvious or even facetious, but there were no markers or road signs over the mountains informing the victorious pioneer that he had indeed made it to the rich lands of Kentucky. The previous year, in 1767, Daniel had set out with his brother Squire and their comrade William Hill up the Big Sandy River in search of Kentucky. Hill was Daniel's friend, frequent hunting companion, and "crony." Nathan Boone later remarked that Hill was "a man after my father's own heart. He was fond of the wilderness, hunting, and wild adventure—a jolly good companion for such a lonely life." Nathan continued in a jocular tone that Hill and Daniel "made an agreement that whoever should die first would return and give the other information about the spirit world. Hill died first, but Father used to say he never received the promised intelligence."[125] In fact, William Hill died shortly after their 1767 journey up Big Sandy.[126]

Believing that Sandy would empty into the Ohio, providing a natural entrance into Kentucky, the three woodsmen crossed the Blue Ridge and Alleghenies in autumn and proceeded to cross the Holston and Clinch rivers near their mountain sources. From there, they reached the Russell Fork of Kentucky's Big Sandy River. They traveled about one hundred miles up its banks, just west of the Cumberland Mountains. Early-nineteenth-century frontier historian George Bancroft asserted, "Streams are the guides which God has set for the stranger in the wilderness" and strangers they were.[127] Although

---

[125] Lofaro, *Daniel Boone.* 25.
[126] Draper, *The Life of Daniel Boone.* 197.
[127] Bancroft, George. *History of the Colonization of United States*. Boston: Charles C Little and James Brown, 1841. 188.

situated near what would later become Young's Salt Works, a meager ten miles due west of modern day Prestonsburg, Floyd County, Kentucky, the weary travelers became disheartened, as they had been "ketched in a snow storm."[128] Lyman Draper writes

> As the country thus far had been forbidding, quite hilly, and much overrun with laurel…they abandoned all hopes of finding Kentucky by this route and made the best of the way back to the Yadkin.[129]

The tired woodsmen, faced by a strong winter storm and perilous conditions, failed to realize that they had made it to Kentucky. Maybe they mistook Sandy's Levisa Fork for the headwaters of the Louisa, which instead placed them many miles outside of Kentucky's borders. Regardless, only a few miles had separated them from the fertile plains and great meadow of legend.

The ironic meeting of these two ingenerate woodsmen in 1768 or 1769 was providential to say the least. Daniel's soul was at a peculiar junction—a turning point. In fact, John Bakeless goes so far to say that Findley "*was* [Daniel's] turning point."[130] Daniel was anxious. On his farm, his family made a meager living and his soul was uneasy. His failed expeditions and land speculations landed him in debt. The Yadkin Valley was teeming with life, but not the life that Daniel sought. Families settled by the day, and land that had been used for hunting and adventurous pleasures twenty years prior was

---

[128] Draper, *The Life of Daniel Boone.* 196; Lofaro, *Daniel Boone.* 25.

[129] Draper, *The Life of Daniel Boone.* 196.

[130] Bakeless, *Daniel Boone.* 46.

steadily domesticated and occupied. Lyman Draper noted that, by 1768, game was "so scare" in the Yadkin "as to render a roast wild turkey or venison steak quite a rarity."[131]

Findley desired to enter Kentucky by land and deeply required the assistance of an experienced woodsman. On the other hand, Daniel, although irked by his recent failures and his restlessness in the Yadkin, could follow any trace and navigate almost anywhere. Fused together, the woodsmen could find and follow the Indian's *Warrior's Path* through the Appalachians and fulfill their "long-cherished ideal of terrestrial beauty and perfection" and finally discover their *Kanta-ke*.[132]

Paradise

On the first of May 1769, an anxious band of woodsman departed Daniel Boone's cabin.[133] Their compass pointed due west and their destination was the horizon. With Daniel in the lead and John Findley close behind, the expedition's team was comprised of Daniel's brother-in-law, John Stuart, as hunter and Joseph Holden, James Mooney, and William Cooley as "camp-keepers."[134] This was a practice that Daniel employed religiously later in life. As long as the trip went to plan, both Daniel and Findley would have little time to "pot-hunt" or prepare the daily skins. Their time in the woods was too valuable. In a sense, this practice was ironic: Daniel's search for the solitude of the West required a community of supporting woodsmen to cook his meat and tan his hides.

---

[131] Draper, *The Life of Daniel Boone.* 207.
[132] Draper, *The Life of Daniel Boone.* 207.
[133] Jackson Independent Patriot, Nov. 8, 1826, pg. 1, col. 1
[134] Bakeless, *Daniel Boone.* 48; Draper, *The Life of Daniel Boone.* 207.

Daniel's brother, Squire Boone, is believed to have stayed on the Yadkin long enough to finish his family's spring planting and caught the party's tracks in late spring. Lyman Draper contended that the party's late departure date in May accounted for Squire's farming needs, although Peter Houston claimed Squire joined the band in late fall after the harvest was complete.[135] In either case, Daniel's soul was set on the horizon and he was not going to wait. Some scholars depict this exodus as a mere hunting trip. Others write that it was a quest for adventure. Some even portray it as a business initiative, due to hard economic times in Northern Carolina. Although such motives may have formed the company's superficial drive, for Daniel, the western excursion was undeniably an outlet for his restless, curious, and famished soul.

Their first task was to scale the mountain chain from Elk Creek to the Blue Ridge and then reach the Three Forks of the New River. Once accomplished the men had to exact their compass to a place dubbed *The Stairs,* a small mountain pass within the greater Stone Mountains. Moving due west, the woodsmen would have invariably struck *The Hunters' Trail,* which led straight for the Cumberland Mountains. Although the trek was incredibly arduous, already hundreds of miles in linear distance through dense forests and high mountains, the men were constant and tirelessly looking straight ahead for the great *Warriors' Path.* With Daniel as their guide, Kentucky was as good as theirs if they could but find the trace.

In short time, perhaps driven by Providence, immense skill, or both, Daniel found it with seeming ease. The party navigated the trace and soon laid eyes upon the legendary gap in the mountains—the hailed white gates of heaven. Robert

---

[135] Houston, *A Sketch of the Life and Character of Daniel Boone.* 1.

Morgan captured this moment, writing that the Cumberland Gap shone as "sharp as a gunsight cut into the mountains."[136] After victoriously crossing through the cut, the band shifted north and passed through Pine Mountain Gap. They would have then crossed the Cumberland River and the Sand Gap—later known as Boone's Gap. The party ultimately settled and established Station Camp—near modern day Irvine, Kentucky.

Daniel appeared to have had little interest in the camp, however. He was eager to ascertain the position of Findley's fabled paradise. Like Thomas of the Bible who needed to see to believe, Daniel needed proof. Alone, he shouldered his rifle and concentrated his gaze toward the waters of the Rockcastle and Kentucky Rivers and climbed the neighboring small mountain—or knob—to gather his position. Upon reaching its commanding height, "towards the time of the setting sun," his heart became light and his soul weightless.[137] Stretching out as far as his eyes could see was the marvelous fact of the true "garden spot of the west."[138] It was *Kanta-ke*.

It is important here to note that Daniel Boone was not the first white man to summit Pilot Knob in order to witness the grandeur of *Kanta-ke*. He was not even the first Yadkin settler, for that matter. A fellow Yadkin frontiersman, Christopher Gist, entered Kentucky by way of the Ohio in April 1750. Gist's mission was to scout the illegal landholdings of the Ohio Company and pacify the Natives within its bounds by asserting that "the English wanted no more from the Indians than trade and friendship."[139] Gist penetrated the Great Meadow's

---

[136] Morgan, *Boone: A Biography.* 96.
[137] Peck, "Life of Daniel Boone." 11.
[138] Draper, *The Life of Daniel Boone.* 211.
[139] Belue, Ted Franklin, *The Long Hunt: Death of the Buffalo east of the Mississippi.* Mechanicsburg: Stackpole Books 1996. 70.

heartland as deep as the Salt River Basin and summited Pilot Knob sometime around February 1751. Concluding his journey, Gist argued that *Kanta-ke's* seemingly virginal land "wants nothing but Cultivation to make it a most delightful Country."[140] The cultivating hand of history soon heard the call.

In his 1812 *Memorial to the Kentucky Legislature,* Daniel wrote that, as he stood alone atop the knob, "which overlooks this terrestrial paradise," he gazed upon "those fertile plains which are unequaled on our earth, and laid the fairest claim to the description of the garden of God."[141] He had wandered in the wilderness for thirty-five years. Now, standing atop the metaphorical Mount Pisgah, Canaan—the land "flowing with milk and honey"—shone brightly before him.

---

[140] Christopher Gist's Journals, ed. William M. Darlingotn (Pittsburgh, 1893), 47.
[141] Boone, Daniel. *Memorial to the Kentucky Legislature.* 1812.

CHAPTER 4

The Piraeus

Weightless, Daniel descended the ridge and entered the Piraeus. After a meditative and nearly religious experience observing the grand cathedrals of *Kanta-ke*, Daniel went off toward camp.[142]

With the help of John Findley and others, Daniel's vision of the great Blue Meadow was now realized. For the next two years, he was fed by her bounties, sometime altogether alone. Towards the end of this great excursion—a true Long Hunt—Daniel, now rejoined with his brother, Squire, and a small band of frontiersmen, journeyed back to the Yadkin. On their return, however, Daniel was captured by the Shawnee warrior, Captain Will Emery, who relieved Daniel's party of all their gear, thirteen horses, many bales of fur, and nine-hundred skins. Sending them on their way, Captain Will beckoned, "Go home, and stay there."[143] Daniel Boone was going home, but he would not stay.

If our mission is to understand the character of Daniel Boone with all its complexities, then this chapter is dedicated to

---

[142] Adapted from Book 1 of Plato's Republic, "I went down to the Piraeus yesterday with Glaucon."
[143] Belue, Ted Franklin, *The Long Hunt.* 102.

both the romantic and the real. Who was Daniel Boone and what can we learn by walking with him through his woods?

. . .

Lyman Draper's exhaustive history described Boone as a "true philosopher."[144] Draper did not mean philosopher in the general sense, however, for Daniel cared little for the wandering thoughts of men. As the Frenchmen Alexis de Tocqueville wrote in Book Two of his work, *Democracy in America,* "Americans have no philosophical school of their own." Tocqueville's argument is undeniably sound, it seems, as America's greatest philosophers were not philosophers at all. Rather, it appears the ranks of American philosophy have always been disguised as storytellers.

Take for instance the works of Mark Twain. In his "Notice" prefacing his great narrative, *The Adventures of Huckleberry Finn,* Twain warned the reader about taking his work too seriously

> Persons attempting to find a motive in this narrative will be prosecuted; persons attempting to find a moral in it will be banished; persons attempting to find a plot in it will be shot. *By Order of the Author.*

Disguised within Twains narrative, however, are his subtle critiques of American society, culture, and democracy. His main character bears the name analogous to an insignificant or unimportant person—Huckleberry.

---

[144] Draper, *The Life of Daniel Boone.* 215.

In his eulogy of Henry David Thoreau, Ralph Waldo Emerson laughs

> Had his genius been only contemplative, he had been fitted to his life, but with his energy and practical ability he seemed born for great enterprise and for command; and I so much regret the loss of his rare powers of action, that I cannot help counting it a fault in him that he had no ambition. Wanting this, instead of engineering for all America, he was the captain of a *huckleberry* party. Pounding beans is good to the end of pounding empires one of these days; but if, at the end of years, it is still only beans!

Twain transported his American philosophy on the back of Huckleberry Finn, a fictional character best known as the uneducated son of a drunkard. Perhaps, Twain's irony is his secret. American philosophy is antithetical to the philosophy of aristocracy and produced not by leisure, as is the case in Europe, but a daily and unique observation and application of the Good, the True, and the Beautiful. In Huck's case, the Common and the Simple. Tocqueville observed a similar maxim

> ...if I seek amongst these characteristics that which predominates over and includes almost all the rest, I discover that in most of the operations of the mind, each American appeals to the individual exercise of his own understanding alone. America is therefore one of the countries in the world where philosophy is least studied, and where the precepts of Descartes are best applied.

It is quite possible that Daniel Boone never heard of René Descartes, read his *Principia Philosophiae,* or understood his famous axiom: *Cogito ergo sum*—translanted, "I think, therefore I am." But Daniel, like Mark Twain, was a storyteller. His story, however distinct from the jocular narratives of Twain, was nevertheless imbued with subtle critiques of culture and society. Although not written in words, Daniel's story was a work of philosophical art, for it was dictated by his curious life and transcribed by his rugged world. Daniel's philosophy was carried by flora and fauna and down the many rivers his journey traversed. It was a very natural philosophy—a First Philosophy and, perhaps, a social philosophy—that was distinguished by one's observations within the purity and sublimity of nature.

Daniel appears to have witnessed with supreme pleasure the pulse of the Western wind, the enigmatic voice of the woods, the sagacity of the tree, the tranquil naivety of the animal, the euphony of the birds. He wrote of his great delights in surveying the fertile valleys and commanding ridges of his *Kanta-ke.* Robert Morgan asserted that Daniel saw "nature as both a fact and a fable, and every cloud and sunset, tree and blade of grass, as instance of both the real and the ideal, physical and spiritual." His philosophic sense of the spiritual was unique among his white contemporaries. Morgan continued, "Every tree and river, rock and cloud, was alive, haunted, significant."[145]

Early Boone historian John Mason Peck writes that Daniel early "acquired the habit of contemplation, and was an enthusiastic admirer of nature in its primeval wildness."[146] He was the first man of his age: an artist and a hunter; a poet and a

---

[145] Morgan, *Boone: A Biography.* 118.
[146] Peck, *Life of Daniel Boone.* 7.

pathfinder; a storyteller and a woodsman. He both defined and exemplified the notion of an "American Adam," the idea that, in America, man was reborn. This rhetoric, not altogether unique to our story, resulted because America was both the land of "thought and action" and of "reflection and choice."[147] It was the old realities of the East mixed with the new and forcefully intimate realities of the American wilderness and its unique vices.

Daniel's thoughts and actions during his own lifetime, let alone those chronicled by the centuries, stirred a peculiar drive in man to crave an ideal nature—an ideal soul. Morgan wrote that such inspiration was because of Daniel's

> Quaker tolerance for others, reliant and integrous, with a large capacity to wonder and reaching out toward the new and mysterious, brave but cautious, sociable, diplomatic, calm in the face of danger.[148]

Lyman Draper asserted a similar maxim

> "He follow[ed] the Ohio—*la Belle Riviere* of the French— in all its silent wanderings—how he sits and studies the huge mountains as they cap their venerable brows with clouds."[149]

Such still meditation and deep observation depict in Daniel a soul of great moral virtue and natural philosophy. He was more

---

[147] The former is derived from Winston Churchill's *My Early Life,* and the latter from Alexander Hamilton's *The Federalist No. One.*

[148] Morgan, *Boone: A Biography.* 118.

[149] Draper, *The Life of Daniel Boone.* 240.

than a hunter and adventurer, and more, perhaps, than an explorer of ancient lands. He has been described as a poet and an artist of the forest, always seeking to understand the secrets beyond the next bluff. Most importantly, however, Daniel Boone was a woodsman-philosopher.

. . .

Robert Morgan noted that "[Daniel] felt an ancient kinship with the forest."[150] Not only could he navigate the woods with extreme ease, he was connected to it. Daniel appeared to feel its great pulse and understand its hushed song. He was one to walk into the morning meadow and hear the silence as it sang.[151] He hungered for its communion. Lyman Draper writes, "No man ever possessed in a more happy combination than Daniel Boone those quiet, taciturn habits, love of solitary adventure, and admiration for the silent charms of nature."[152] He concluded that, as "new groves and woods and hills and plains salute[d] his vision with each returning dawn," the soul of Daniel Boone was wonderfully nourished by the "perfectly delicious" and sublime frontier.[153]

Daniel's soul rejoiced under its wondrous canopy. Legend has it that, in 1770, a group of hunters ventured into Kentucky, led by Kaspar Mansker, the first true European longhunter in the American West. As they crept silently amidst Kentucky's dark night, a faint song pierced the darkness. With his musket loaded and primed, Mansker slowly approached the

---

[150] Morgan, *Boone: A Biography.* 79.
[151] This phrase is taken from *I Won't Be Found,* by the Tallest Man on Earth.
[152] Draper, *The Life of Daniel Boone.* 229.
[153] Draper, *The Life of Daniel Boone.* 239.

melody and feared the worst. Perhaps they had stumbled upon a Cherokee war party and would have to fight their way out. To his great surprise, what Mansker saw was a man, "flat upon his back, and singing at the top of his voice."[154] His bed was deerskin and his entertainment the night sky. He was entirely alone, but wholeheartedly happy. He was Daniel Boone.

An early dispatch from Fort Osage, reprinted in *Niles' Register* in 1816, asserted that Daniel, who "might have accumulated riches as readily as any man in Kentucky," preferred "the woods, where you see him in the dress of the roughest, poorest hunter."[155] Although Ralph Waldo Emerson was yet to be born, the life of Daniel Boone exemplified the ideal harmony with nature that Emerson would later write about

> The sun illuminates only the eye of the man, but shines into the eye and the heart of the child. The lover of nature is he whose inward and outward senses are still truly adjusted to each other; who has retained the spirit of infancy even into the era of manhood. His intercourse with heaven and earth becomes part of his daily food. In the presence of nature a wild delight runs through the man, in spite of real sorrows."[156]

Daniel was such a child in spirit. As though the mind of Emerson and the life of Boone transcended time, Daniel would write of his time alone in Kentucky, "I was surrounded by plenty in the midst of want; I was happy in the midst of dangers and

---

[154] Faragher, *Daniel Boone.* 85.
[155] Niles' Register, X, 361 (June 15, 1816).
[156] Emerson, Ralph Waldo. "Nature" in *Selected Essays, Lectures, and Poems.* Robert D. Richardson Jr., ed. New York: Bantam Dell, 1990. 18.

inconveniences. In such a diversity, it was impossible I should be disposed to melancholy."

Daniel's 1775 wilderness companion, Felix Walker, summed up their romantic perceptions of the pure West, writing

> Nothing can furnish the contemplative mind with more sublime reflections, than nature unbroken by art; we can there trace the wisdom of the Great Architect in the construction of his work in nature's simplicity, which, when he had finished, he pronounced all good.[157]

Like Emerson, Daniel fervently sought to "interrogate the great apparition that shines so peacefully around" him and zealously inquired "to what end is nature?" Like Emerson, Daniel was captivated by the true "City of God"—the "heavenly bodies" (stars)—as "one might think the atmosphere was made transparent with this design, to give man, in the heavenly bodies, the perpetual presence of the sublime." Like Emerson, Daniel understood that nature "reflect[s] the wisdom of his best hour" as it "delight[s]" in the "simplicity of his childhood."[158] But, unlike Emerson, Daniel's woods was more than philosophical. In the woods, Daniel was a true American philosopher—he was a storyteller.

Perhaps Daniel's childhood in nature is more akin to that of Emerson's pupil, Henry David Thoreau. Entering his wondrous essay, *Walking*, Thoreau penned, "I wish to speak a word for Nature, for absolute freedom and wildness." Thoreau's

---

[157] Walker, Felix. *Felix Walker's Narrative of His Trip with Boone from Long Island to Boonesborough in March 1775.* Debow's Review of February, 1854. 4.
[158] Emerson, *Selected Essays.* 17.

uniquely American philosophy centered on the healing and constructive power of "regarding man as an inhabitant ... of nature" and not "a member of society." Robert Morgan argued that "Thoreau put into sentences the poetry and thought Boone had lived."[159] Like Daniel, Thoreau believed that the "future lies [in the West]." In such a vast wilderness—for that is what Thoreau meant by the West—humanity would find its "preservation."[160] But it was Daniel that actually walked West.

Daniel's natural philosophy nurtured problematic results, however. The further his love of the raw, untouched, and uncultivated world drove his exploration, the more open and visible the western path became. Although Daniel held nature as "a series of wonders, and a fund of delight," his presence therein appeared to reduce its awe and bankrupt its sublimity, for his path would be forever connected with empire.

The histories written of Daniel Boone throughout the mid-to-late nineteenth century embrace him as their archetypal pioneer-hero. These writers paint their myth-heroes according to the problematic canvas of Western-ism, meaning the "desirability of the West as a place to live absolutely in terms of the idea of progress," According to historian James K. Folsom. He continued

> "To [them], life in the West becomes more desirable as conditions in the West itself approach conditions in the East; and [their] hope for the future of the West is that hit

---

[159] Morgan, *Boone: a Biography.* xviii.
[160] Walden, Chapter 1, *Writings,* Riverside edition, 11 vols. (Boston, 1893-1894), II, 21-23, 25-28.

will someday equal, or indeed surpass, the East in strictly Eastern value of civilized comfort."[161]

In the opening lines of his 1856 biography *Daniel Boone and the Hunters of Kentucky*, William Henry Bogart declared

> If it be fame, that in the progress of a great empire, one name above all others be associated with its deliverance from the dominion of the savage…then this inheritance is that of the subject of this memoir—Daniel Boone."[162]

Bogart concluded that it was Boone's providential destiny to lead the American nation "to its place of power."

Moreover, Timothy Flint's 1833 *Biographical Memoir of Daniel Boone* painted Boone as civilization's godfather and "a willing servant of society, proud of his role as pathfinder for the more sophisticated social order which will follow him."[163] Although a lover of the pure wilderness, Daniel is remembered as its greatest conqueror.

Famously, Frederick Jackson Turner would write in the late nineteenth century that Boone's discovery of the Cumberland Gap—really, his popularization of its great V-Shaped notch—paved wide a gateway for the East to expire the primordial West. He believed that Boone epitomized the white advancement across the American continent. "Stand at Cumberland Gap," Turner wrote, "and watch the procession of

---

[161] Flint, *Biographical Memoir of Daniel Boone*. 10.

[162] Bogart, William Henry. *Daniel Boone and the Hunters of Kentucky*. Boston: Lee and Shepard, 1875. 13.

[163] Flint, *Biographical Memoir of Daniel Boone*. 13.

civilization, marching single file...and the frontier has passed by."

Turner's presentation of Boone as civilization's pathfinder and way-maker was not unique among nineteenth-century cultural or political critiques. Fifty years before Turner's thesis, Missouri artist George C. Bingham painted his most famous work, *Daniel Boone Escorting Settlers Through the Cumberland Gap*. Hanging today at Washington University's art museum, the painting's title speaks volumes. With his archaic ancient Greek smile, Boone leads a band of settlers through the great Gap. On the right of the painting, the harrowing remains of a tree loom in the shadows. Its limbs and trunk look as though they were blasted by the modern weapons of war. Boone stands firms in the center of the painting, as he holds the reigns of a white horse, on top of which sits a woman. She is clad in a simple shall and rides sidesaddle. She is civilization and Boone is leading the way.

Boone as civilization's conquering pathfinder was not his only historical presentation, however. The eighth canto of *Don Juan* presents a different image of our woodsman, however. Lord Byron suspended his discussion of the siege of Ismail to discuss Daniel Boone, the "back-woodsman of Kentucky." Byron described Boone as an altruistic and simple man. Most importantly, however, Byron's depiction painted the old woodsman as a "child of Nature,"[164] whose "virtues shames the corruptions of civilization," writes Henry Nash Smith.[165] Lord Byron wrote

---

[164] *Don Juan,* Canto 8.
[165] Smith, *Virgin Land.* 55.

> For killing nothing but a bear or buck, he
> Enjoy'd the lonely, vigorous, harmless days
> Of his old age in wilds of deepest maze.
>
> . . .
>
> The inconvenience of civilization
> Is, that you neither can be pleased nor please;
> But where he met the individual man,
> He show'd himself as kind as mortal can.
>
> ...
>
> The free-born forest found and kept [him] free,
> And fresh as is a torrent or a tree.

Regardless of Lord Byron's idealized depiction, Boone's paradox remains. Although the "free-born forest" both pleased and freed Boone, its purity, simplicity, and sublimity steadily diminished as Boone's adventures expanded.

But Daniel Boone was not alone. The nineteenth century poet and journalist Walt Whitman also struggled the clash between civilization and savagery, between cultivated man and primitive nature. Whitman's poetry is imbued with both a particular adoration for nature's cultivation and a peculiar longing for the perpetuation of the rawness of its pure sublimity. Whitman believed that, as the budding American Republic grew, so must it distance itself from its "feudal past of Europe" and build its foundation upon the order of nature.[166] In *Poems of the Sayers of the Words of the Earth*, Whitman wrote

---

[166] Ward, John William. *Andrew Jackson—Symbol for an Age*. London: Oxford University Press, 1953. page 44.

I swear there is no greatness or power that does not emulate those of the earth! I swear there can be no theory of any account, unless it corroborates the theory of the earth! No politics, art, religion, behavior, or what not, is of account, unless it compares with the amplitude of the earth, unless it face the exactness, vitality, impartiality, rectitude of the earth.[167]

Whitman's flight from feudalism found its home in the American West. He believed that America's political foundation must rest on the "exactness, vitality, impartiality…and rectitude" of nature. Perhaps Whitman saw America's Eastern Seaboard as a luminous shadow of her European and cultivated past or, simultaneously, perhaps he was captivated by the beauty and vigor of the wild.

In either scenario, Whitman appeared to understand the health of American society as dependent upon the healthy future of its untainted West. He concluded his most celebrated poem, *Pioneers! O Pioneers,* praising the westward army of frontiersmen

Till with sound of trumpet,
Far, far off the day-break call—hark! How loud and clear it hear it wind;
Swift! To the head of the army!—swift! Spring to your places, Pioneers! O pioneers.[168]

Describing the rugged frontiersmen as members of an army, with trumpets that take the wind and swift movements that bring

---

[167] Whitman, Walt. "Poem of the Sayers of the Words of the Earth," *Leaves of Grass.* (New York, 1856). p. 329.
[168] Whitman, Walt. *Pioneers! O Pioneers!* Stanza 26

order to the unordered, Whitman's portrayal of westward movement was paradoxical. In one sense, it was natural, as the children of Adam have drifted westward through history. But it was also forced, as though the savage and untouched wilderness required the conquering and subduing of an army.

In Whitman's *Song of Myself,* which has been described as a true representation of "the core of [his] poetic vision,"[169] his words take on a new tone

> The friendly and flowing savage, who is he?
> Is he waiting for civilization, or past it and mastering it?
> Is he some Southwesterner rais'd out-doors? is he Kanadian?
> Is he from the Mississippi country? Iowa, Oregon, California?
> The mountains? prairie-life, bush-life? or sailor from the sea?
>
> Wherever he goes men and women accept and desire him,
> They desire he should like them, touch them, speak to them, stay with them.
> Behavior lawless as snow-flakes, words simple as grass, uncomb'd head, laughter, and naiveté,
> Slow-stepping feet, common features, common modes and emanations,
> They descend in new forms from the tips of his fingers,
> They are wafted with the odor of his body or breath, they fly out of the glance of his eyes.

Whitman praises him who is beyond civilization, whose society is that of the snowflake and language that of nature. He

---

[169] Greenspan, Ezra, ed. *Walt Whitman's "Song of Myself": A Sourcebook and Critical Edition.* New York: Routledge, 2005. Print.

exemplifies the ideal American man as not one who is averse to law and language, but one who has developed a higher form of logic and reason—that of nature.

Expounding further, Whitman writes

I hear you whispering there O stars of heaven,
O suns—O grass of graves—O perpetual transfers and promotions,
If you do not say any thing how can I say any thing?[170]

Whitman makes clear his belief that the voice of nature supplies the power of thought to mankind. But in Whitman's own thoughts, the paradox and question of the early American West is encumbered by his vision of a frontier army. Was the West a land to be conquered by the strength and resolve of a pioneers? Or, was it a pure and already perfected land to be left alone? Whitman's poetry appears insufficient for the task, as he leaves this question entirely unanswered, and maybe for good reason.

The Father of the National Park System also struggled with this problem. John Muir was an environmental philosopher and "shaped the very categories through which thoughtful Americans understand and envision" their West and their responsible "relationships with [that] natural world."[171] In many ways, the history and mission of Muir was to save the "American soul from total surrender to materialism," writes Muir historian Donald Worster. Whatever his focus, Muir's vision of the West is complex and incomplete, although romantic and real.

---

[170] *Walt Whitman's "Song of Myself.".*Stanza 49.
[171] Holmes, Steven (1999). *The Young John Muir: An Environmental Biography.* Madison: Univ. of Wisconsin Press.

In his 1897 essay, *The American Forests*, Muir lamented

> Through all the wonderful, eventful centuries since Christ's time—and long before that—God has cared for these trees, saved them from drought, disease, avalanches, and a thousand straining, leveling tempests and floods; but he cannot save them from fools.[172]

Muir compared this fool with a rich "spendthrift" who "inherited a magnificent estate in perfect order," and then left it to be "sold and plundered and wasted at will." Unlike his contemporaries, who painted the American pioneer as the hero, Muir contended that they were its destroyers, who spread "death and confusion in the fairest…gardens ever planted."

> Any fool can destroy trees. They cannot run away; and if they could, they would still be destroyed,—chased and hunted down as long as fun or a dollar could be got out of their bark hides.[173]

But Muir also understood land use; that nature provides only as much as it is provided for. Alongside this fool, Muir argued that "no place is too good for good men." Muir seemingly understood that opportunity existed in the natural world for those who cared enough to see it and to attract it. His diversion from other writers occurs not in the tone of his many

---

[172] Muir, John, "The American Forests," in *John Muir: Nature Writings.* William Cronon, ed., New York: Library of America, 1997. 720.

[173] Muir, John, "The American Forests." 720.

narratives, but in character of *his* pioneer. The Western "ground" was "happy to feed" responsible setters, those who took enough and not too much, but it was impoverished by those, "destroyers, tree-killers, wool and mutton men," who took without control. In other words, Muir declared, "few destroyers of trees ever plant any." [174]

From Muir's perspective, it was not the Western hero but the hero within the West that would shape America's positive legacy. Muir's problem is the problem of man, for, after all his rhetoric, Muir lamented, "Only Uncle Sam can" preserve the Western forests.

. . .

But the tough question remains for us. How did Daniel Boone understand himself and his role in civilization's wooded periphery? Was he a "good man," or someone who used nature for mere economic gain? It would be natural for the founder of the Western path to be proud of his achievement, to look behind him and find the steady advance of a prospering civilization following his footprints. In Boone's case, this was not so.

An anonymous kinsman wrote, "like the unrefined Savage," Daniel "certainly prefere[d] a state of nature to a state of Civilization."[175] Just as Daniel's soul longed for an intimate communion with the forest, his person as an individual in human society desired a cozy connection with his surroundings. Henry Nash Smith dubbed orderly human civilization—the East—as "pernicious...because it interposes a veil of

---

[174] Muir, John, "Save the Redwoods," in *John Muir: Nature Writings.* William Cronon, ed., New York: Library of America, 1997. 830.
[175] Smith, *Virgin Land.* 55.

artificiality between the individual and the natural objects of experience." Smith equated the "sophisticated art" of civilization as the unnatural substitute for the "realities of things."[176] Thomas J. Farnham, an early-nineteenth-century explorer and writer, wrote that, while some boast of civilization's triumph, others scorn the aid of science and "look through Nature, without the aid of science, up to its causes."[177] Daniel Boone appears to be such a man.

After his 1818 interview with the aged woodsman—just a year or so before Boone's death—John Mason Peck writes that "[Boone's] most prominent traits of his character were unshaken fortitude and self-command." After sitting in the Boone's home and conversing with him for many hours, Peck traveled back East to write his book. When Peck originally began his journey West to meet and interview Daniel, he intended to find a strong-willed hunter-hero. Instead, he found a simple man imbued with a love of nature, its solitude and all its wondrous glories—he found a philosopher in the woods.

Peck writes that Daniel, being "accustomed to be much alone in the woods," developed "the habit of contemplation and was an enthusiastic admirer of nature in its primeval wilderness." He continued, "Throughout his whole life," Daniel felt a strong "repugnance to the technical forms of law and the conventional regulations of society and of governments."[178]

Ironically, nineteenth-century biographer William H. Bogart agreed, although the overall tone of his history presents our Boone as the triumphant conqueror of unknown lands.

---

[176] Smith, *Virgin Land.* 72.
[177] Thomas J. Farnham, *Travels in the Great Western Prairies, the Anahuac and Rocky Mountains, and in the Oregon Territory* (Poughkeepsie, N. Y., 1841), p. 72.
[178] Peck, *Life of Daniel Boone.* 7.

Bogart writes, "All [Daniel's]…history shows that he had no attachment for the perpetual society of humanity."[179] If given his druthers, it appears that Daniel would have answered that his love lay in the primordial West, and he would prefer to simply lie under its sublime canopy on his deerskins and sing.

In his 1846 editions of the *North American Review,* James H. Perkins was the first to portray Daniel as a "white Indian," who ventured into the wilderness not to find wealth or fame, but because of "a love of nature, of perfect freedom, and of the adventurous life in the woods." Perkins continued

[Daniel Boone] would have pined and died as a nabob in the midst of civilization. He wanted a frontier, and the perils and pleasures of a frontier life, not wealth; and he was happier in his log-cabin, with a loin of venison and his ramrod for a spit, than he would have been amid the greatest profusion of modern luxuries."[180]

In a 1796 letter to Governor Isaac Shelby—the first governor of the State of Kentucky and previous surveyor of Boonesborough in 1775-1776—Daniel himself remarked, "I am no Statesman I am a Woodsman"[181] Although he opened the West to the common man and, although he would be forever depicted as the great American pioneer, Daniel Boone was a highly simplistic, solitude-loving woodsman-philosopher, driven forever to marvel at the setting sun and uncover the mysteries laying beyond the next ridge.

[179] Bogart, William Henry. *Daniel Boone and the Hunters of Kentucky.* Boston: Lee and Shepard, 1875. 32.
[180] Perkins, James H. *North American Review*, LXII, 97, 86-87. (January, 1846).
[181] Collins, Lewis. *History of Kentucky*, 1877. vol ii, p. 242.

CHAPTER 5

High Wind Rising

Bygone Symbols of a Proud Age

In 1838, the summer sun burned the soul of the Cherokee and the fiery irons of American hypocrisy heated up for their marking task. Although no Cherokee officers or their leader, John Ross, signed the infamous "Treaty of New Echota," the children of the soil packed their huddled masses into internment camps to prepare for their long and forced journey West. *Junaluska*, the leader of the Eastern Band of the Cherokee Indians who saved Andrew Jackson's life during the 1814 Creek War Campaign in the battle of Horseshoe Bend, was himself arrested when he tried to travel to Washington to reason with his old friend. But President Jackson passed the treaty and replied, "Sir, your audience is ended, there is nothing I can do for you." *Junaluska* was to be deported with the rest of his Cherokee brothers. "If I would had known that Jackson would drive us from our homes, I would have killed him at the Horseshoe," he later wrote.[182]

---

[182] Williams, Paul. *Jackson, Crockett, and Houston on the American Frontier.* Jefferson: McFarland & Company, Inc., 2016. 121

John Quincy Adams described the treaty as an "eternal disgrace upon the country," and the English traveler Frances Trollope argued

> ...declaimed upon in Congress, roared out in taverns, discussed in every drawing room, satirized upon the stage, nay, even anathematized from the pulpit: listen to it, and then look at them at home; you will them with one hand hoisting the cap of liberty, and with the other ... driving from their homes the children of the soil, whom they have bound themselves to protect by the most solemn treaties ... Strong indeed must the love of equality in an English breast if it can survive a tour through the Union.[183]

Some would die in the summer camps from exposure and disease; some would die on the winter journey itself. Nearly half of the thirteen thousand men, women, and children would perish before the tired, poor, and breathless last completed the Trail of Tears.

In his 1836 letter to the American President, Ralph Waldo Emerson pleaded for justice

> Such a dereliction of all faith and virtue, such a denial of justice, and such deafness to screams for mercy were never heard of in times of peace and in the dealing of a nation with its own allies and wards, since the earth was made. ... You, sir, will bring down that renowned chair in which you sit into infamy if your seal is set to this instrument of

---

[183] Williams, Stanley T. "The Founding of Main Street: The Letters of Mrs. Trollope," in *The North American Review,* Volume 215. New York: North American Review Corporation, 1922. 778.

perfidy; and the name of this nation, hitherto the sweet omen of religion and liberty, will stink to the world.

Putrid, Jackson enforced his Indian removal policy regardless.

The Cherokee name was given to them by European settlers centuries before and now these plump settlers were taking it away. Originally, the Cherokee called themselves the Ani-Yunwiya, or, DɦBƟ⬿, the "Principal People." Long before Romulus and Remus or the burst of Western civilization, the Principal People lived, farmed, and hunted the land they were now ejected from. Although they had long lost the struggle to control the European germ in their Eastern periphery, the Native American remained a visible symbol of a bygone and proud age. But now, under the scorching summer sun of 1838, the Ani-Yunwiya ceased to exist, for the civilized ideals of the advancing American mind had killed them.

The Lockean Mistake

The modern professor of environmental biology and a member of the Potawatomi Nation, Robin Wall Kimmerer writes, "The arrogance of English is its underlying assumption that the only way to be animate," to be alive, and to be "worthy of respect and moral concern, is to be human."[184] John Locke would have tack on "civilized" in addition to "human."

In his *Second Treatise on Government*, Locke argued, "In the beginning all the World was America."[185] From Locke's

---

[184] Robin Wall Kimmerer, "Learning the Grammar of Animacy," in *Colors of Nature: Culture, Identity, and the Natural World.* Alison H Deming & Lauret E. Savor, ed., Minneapolis: Milkweed Editions, 2011. 176.
[185] John Locke, *Two Treatises of Government*, Peter Laslett, ed., Cambridge Texts in the History of Ideas, Cambridge, 1988, Treatise II, para. 49.

perspective, the New World represented an historical *tabula rasa*—the historical beginnings of man. It's seemingly boundless and primordial land was, in a sense, Locke's creation story: his political account of Genesis and Britain's opportunity for a second Eden.

Locke believed that the New World yearned for the colonizing and enlightening force of civil society to awaken the "darkness...on the face of [its] deep."[186] Although he is credited as the Father of Liberalism, Locke strongly argued for the colonization of America—a seemingly incompatible pairing. Its opportunity represented a biblically and morally flawed but politically advantageous two-fold creation account. It was an open and pristine land to both witness first-hand the origins of mankind's natural past as well as a land to receive the promise of civilized man's seemingly boundless and deeply enlightened future.

The foundation of Locke's second Eden, however, crumbles under questioning. How can Locke's liberal political philosophy—based on the deep Libertas of humanity—invade and conquer by force and dominance? If mankind was not born "with saddles on their backs," to quote one of Locke's greatest students, then how could he argue that Britain, by right, "was the favored few booted and spurred" who were "ready to ride them legitimately, by the grace of god?"[187]

Locke's answer was simple. The Natives of America are not organized under political societies and their primitive state of nature—their lack of order, law, agriculture, and permanence—demanded a colonizing and civilizing force. Locke's rhetoric removes the European invasion of the

---

[186] Genesis 1:2, NKJV
[187] Thomas Jefferson Letter to Roger Weightman.

Americas from the historical arena and reduces European conquest into a mechanical process. In a sense, one could argue that Locke's arguments were based in compassion and Christian charity—the Europeans were here to help. But this is not my argument.

Locke's creation story lacks enlightenment, as the New World was neither new nor was it a second Eden. It has been a longstanding belief that the ancestors of the Natives came to the American continent across the Bering Strait nearly thirteen thousand years ago. They maintained small, nomadic and isolated groups and impacted little the surrounding country for millennia. They were, in a sense, a forgotten people, swallowed up by the vastness of the pristine and primordial wilderness that they seemingly entered into by accident. Their peripatetic tale is one that resembles the animalistic proclivities of nature itself— where their effects are intimately rugged and ultimately distant from civil society.

However, recent geological, archeological, and historical analysis and findings suggest that the Natives of America were here far longer than we originally thought and swarmed this hemisphere with piercingly intense and decidedly purposeful numbers. In fact, their presence effected such significant and imposing changes in the landscape that, from his flagship, the Santa Maria, Columbus would have witnessed a world systematically and fully marked by mankind. The eastern Natives built roads, canals, dikes, mounds, and reservoirs, alongside elevated and highly-managed agricultural fields. They developed food forests that we are still enjoying and reaping benefits from today. They were, in their own way, highly sophisticated in the arts and sciences, maintained complex political systems, and deeply impacted the world around them.

The world Columbus witnessed was not, as the Smithsonian Institute declared in *Seeds of Change: Christopher Columbus and the Columbian Legacy,* an "Eden, a pristine natural kingdom," where the "native people were transparent in the landscape, living as natural elements of the ecosphere."[188] Geographer William Denevan termed this overtly Edenic and pure outlook as "the pristine myth"—the belief that, "in 1492," the "Americas were a sparsely populated wilderness, -a world of barely perceptible human disturbance."[189] To understand Locke's mistake, therefore, we must first understand the foundations and resultant narratives of this mythology.

The Pristine Myth

Our consideration here is more than simply academic. Behind Locke's creation story lurks the justification of European invasion and the Native's removal—the irresistible narrative that erases the aboriginal and frames the toppling force of progress as inevitable. Was the colonial contest of the New World simply mechanical, a kind of operatic tragedy, or was it historical, where real actors are "morally accountable for their actions," as historian James Wilson writes?[190]

Locke's myth impacted millions of lives, a world empire, and over six hundred years of history. If the Natives of America deftly used and seriously impacted their local ecology,

---

[188] Shetler, Stanwyn. "Three faces of Eden, " In *Seeds of change: A Quincentennial Commemoration,* ed. H. J. Viola and C. Margolis. Washington: Smithsonian Institution Press, 1997. 226.

[189] Denevan, William M. "The Pristine Myth: The Landscape of the Americas in 1492," in *Annals of the Association of American Geographers,* Vol. 82, No. 3. Oxfordshire: Taylor & Francis, Ltd., 1992. 369.

[190] Wilson, James. *The Earth Shall Weep: A History of Native America,* New York: Atlantic Monthly Press, 1998. Prologue.

if their term on this land was old and established, and if they organized themselves into stable, political and sustainable societies that were governed by laws and were dedicated to protecting and preserving the common good, then the "innocent" and Christian foundations of European colonization crumble at their base. Were the Natives a people worthy of rights, or were they something else?

In his eighteenth-century work, *The Law of Nations,* Emer de Vattel argued

> The whole earth is destined to furnish sustenance for its inhabitants; but it can not do this unless it be cultivated. [Therefore] while the conquest of the civilized Empires of Peru and Mexico was a notorious usurpation, the establishment of various colonies upon the continent of North America might, if done within just limits, have been entirely lawful. The people of those vast tracts of land rather roamed over them than inhabited them.[191]

Let us employ the rhetoric of the conquerors to unchain the rights of the conquered. In the naivety and humility of this place, we can learn about the Native inhabitants' rich culture and impact to our story.

The moral and political validity of European invasion is dependent on the validity of the pristine myth. If the Natives of America willingly "joyn[ed] in Society with others who [were] already united, or have a mind to unite for the mutual *Preservation* of their Lives, *Liberties* and *Estates* (Property)," then they were, in fact, civilized by Locke's very definition, and

---

[191] Vattel, Emer de. *The Law of Nations or the Principles of Natural Law.* Washington: The Carnegie Institute of Washington, 1916. 38.

their removal was an act of war—not charity.[192] But let us begin with the myth.

John Locke was not alone in his beliefs and should not carry the entirety of the blame for this theory. He never visited the New World and relied on the writings of European explorers, philosophers, and conquerors. The concept of the Noble Savage dates back to Bartolome de Las Casas' 1530 ethnography, *Apologética Historia Sumaria.* Las Casas argued that the American Natives were "natural creatures," who, in their "prelapsarian innocence...had been quietly waiting...for Christian instruction."[193] Moreover, in 1556, Pietro Martire d'Anghiera argued that the Native

> Seeme to lyve in that goulden worlde of the which owlde wryters speake so much: wherein men lyved simplye and innocentlye without inforcement of lawes, without quarellinge Judges and libelles, contente onely to satisfie nature, without further vexation for knowelege of things to come.

This view lasted three millennia.

In 1835, the American historian George Bancroft wrote of the Native American. He argued that, prior to Columbus, North America was "an unproductive waste...Its only inhabitants were a few scattered tribes of feeble barbarians, destitute of commerce and of political connection."[194] From Las Casas to Bancroft, the Natives were perceived as existing outside of change and by in no way effected it. Because of either

---

[192] John Locke, *Two Treatises of Government*, sTreatise II, para. 123.
[193] Mann, Charles, C. *1491: New Revelations of the America Before Columbus.* New York: Vintage Books: 2005. 15.
[194] Bancroft, George. "History of the United States from the Discovery of the American Continent, Volume 1." Oxford: Oxford University, 1854, 4.

laziness or innocence, the Natives of the New World appeared to have lived in a way that caused little environmental impact to the world around them.

Twentieth-century American historian and anthropologist Alfred L Kroeber argued in his *Cultural and Natural Areas of Native North American* that Native societies in the American East would not have "led to anything in the way of economic or social benefit nor of increase of numbers." Kroeber argued that, in the "absence of all effective political organization" and "economic classes," Native life remained "stationary" and, therefore, "unstable." Kroeber contributed these claims to the "fact" that the Native's impact on their surrounding ecology was minimal, if not entirely nonexistent. He claimed, "Ninety-nine per cent or more of what might have been developed remained virgin, and was tolerated...as waste intervening to the nearest enemy."[195] The purpose of the Native, argued one British historian, "is to show to the present an image of the past from which by history it has escaped." If history is change and civilized human action is the impacting force, then the Natives were a people without history and entirely wretched.

The Natives of the New World were seemingly perfect examples of Locke's philosophical Savage Man, who lived in harmony with the collective laws of nature and as the "absolute Lord of his own Person and Possessions." They were viewed as natural and innocent creatures and were comparable to the animals they hunted. They foraged to live and moved when the forage moved. Like the European's domesticated cow, the Natives of the New World required the Old World's saving and preserving influence. Today must always yield to tomorrow.

---

[195] Kroeber, Aldred Louis. *Cultural and Natural Areas of Native North America.* Berkeley: University Of California Press, 1963. 149-150.

Locke and his enlightened collogues thought it natural that, if mankind's Enjoyment of Freedom was "very uncertain, and constantly exposed to the Invasion of others," then the "great and chief end" of all proper human society is the "preservation of their Property."[196] How could the seemingly nomadic and unorganized Native be civilized? In his *Second Treatise,* Locke laid out the preliminary foundations of such preserving society as needing common laws, indifferent judges, and the power of executive action.

Science and the human will are dangerous powers. Throughout the past two centuries, mankind's ability to understand more completely its past has continuously developed. Today, new disciplines and technology are leading the way to understanding our past. In his revolutionary book, *1491: New Revelations of the Americas Before Columbus,* Charles Mann postulates that

> Demography, climatology, epidemiology, economics, botany, and palynology' molecular and evolutionary biology; carbon-14 dating, ice-core sampling, satellite photography, and soil assays; genetic microsatellite analysis and virtual 3-D fly-throughs ... [show] a new picture of the Americas and their original inhabitants
>
> .

Mann concludes that, opposed to the long-standing belief, the American Natives

> were not nomadic, but built up and lived in some of the world's biggest and most opulent cities. Far from being dependent on big-game hunting, most Indians lived on

---

[196] John Locke, *Two Treatises of Government*, Treatise II, para. 123.

farms…In other words, the Americas were immeasurably busier, more diverse, and more populous than researchers had previously imagined … and older, too.[197]

After years of study, it appears that not only did Natives organize on a large scale, but they also dramatically transformed their surrounding ecosystems. Their modes of animal husbandry and holistic land management predate European or "enlightened" methods by hundreds of years. Rather than domesticating animals, some Native tribes "retooled ecosystems to encourage" wild animals to thrive and live close by. They scorched the thick forest's undergrowth to both encourage herbivores and protect the people who ate them. Instead of building fences, they encouraged predators. It was a deeply regenerative system of agriculture, and it was overlooked. Mann explained

> Rather than the thick, unbroken, monumental snarl of trees imagined by Thoreau, the great eastern forest was an ecologically kaleidoscope of garden plots, blackberry rambles, pine barrens, and specious groves of chestnut, hickory, and oak. [198]

Yes, today must always yield to tomorrow, but we have much to learn.

---

[197] Mann, Charles, C. *1491*. 18.
[198] Mann, Charles, C. *1491*. 286.

Introduction To Our West

The American frontier was a land of rivers and mountains and of infinite horizons. Pulitzer Prize winner, Kiowa writer, and poet N. Scott Momaday described it as a "land of sacred realties—powerful things." He continued, "It's a landscape that has to be seen to be believed and I say on an occasion it may have to be believed to be seen." Most importantly, it *was* a powerful reality, for it possessed a seemingly endless ability to attract and to define, to seize and to liberate. The American frontier of our story *is* the contested periphery of Anglo-Native settlement. This living topography was the meeting ground of Western civilization and the true West—where the backcountry collided with Indian country.

In his 1947 environmental and geographical survey of the native cultures of North America, Kroeber described the eighteenth-century frontier as "a new, assimilated, hybrid-Caucasian culture." In turn, the American pioneers of the day were often branded as hybrid-Indians.[199] The more intense the collision, the less distinguishable each culture became. Historian R. Davis Edmunds concluded that, by 1800, "the Shawnee way of life represented a combination of aboriginal and European cultures."[200]

Late-eighteenth-century Presbyterian minister David McClure concurred in his observations, writing, "At the aptly named Newcomer's Town in 1772," he "found traditional bark longhouses adjacent to backcountry-style log cabins." The Delaware prophet Neolin's home stands as a great example.

---

[199] Kroeber, Alfred Louis. *Cultural and Natural Areas of Native North America*, Volume 38, page 90.
[200] Edmunds, R. David. *Tecumseh and the Quest for Indian Leadership*. 2nd Edition, Mark C Carnes, ed., New York: Person Longman, 2007. 57.

McClure observed that, although a prophet of times past, Neolin's home had a "stone cellar, staircase, stone chimney, fireplace, closets, and apartments (rooms)" that all reminded him of "an English dwelling."[201] It is clear that, as the Native's dependence on the outside world increased, so also their amazing cultural uniqueness proportionally receded into the lost periphery of history.

Richard Slotkin argued that the evolution of American Western mythology was the evolution of the American mind's "too-slow awakening to the significance of the American Indian in the universal scheme of things generally and in our American world in particular."[202] Therefore, to understand Daniel Boone's thoughts of—and actions within—the natural and culturally mixed world of the American West, we must first understand the collision and its resulting turbulence.

On Natural Civilization

Archeological evidence suggests the "continual presence" of Native Americans on the south side of the Ohio River for "ten thousand years prior to the arrival of Europeans."[203] When the first white explorers entered Ohio's fertile river valley, the number and magnitude of monumental earthworks lining the riverbanks perplexed them. Southwest of the valley, they unearthed mummified human remains and uncovered many other artifacts of prehistoric life. They found

---

[201] Franklin B. Dexter, ed., *Diary of David McClure, Doctor of Divinity, 1748-1820* (New York, 1899), 68.

[202] Slotkin, *Regeneration Through Violence.* 17.

[203] Aaron, *How the West Was Lost.* 6.

evidence of aged and ordered civilizations; evidence of communities, organized religion, and political life.

The valley's Late Prehistoric Period (1000 AD – 1650 AD) was a time of change and solidification, witnessing great modifications in "subsistence, settlement, and social structure."[204] In his Archeological survey of the Ohio country, Bradley Lepper writes that the changes in the Late Prehistoric Period included

> A shift to larger and more permanent villages, changes in the form and construction of ceramic vessels, changing ritual practices, increasing evidence for institutionalized leaders, and a dramatic increase in the use of maize as a staple food.[205]

Maize—or Indian corn—was cultivated; peoples settled and began dwelling in established villages; egalitarian tribes cemented into organized and hierarchal political bodies. This period was also categorized as a time of relative peace and improvement.

In Query XI of his *Notes on the State of Virginia,* Thomas Jefferson documented his own excavations of an Indian "barrow"—or gravesite. Finding what he believed to be over one thousand skeletons, Jefferson discovered no battle wounds or "holes" in any of them.[206] Modern archeological records of

---

[204] Robert A Genheimer, ed., "Cultures Before Contact: The Late Prehistory of Ohio and Surrounding Regions" in *Ohio Archaeological Council,* 2000.

[205] Lepper, T. Bradley. *Ohio Archeology: An Illustrated Chronicle of Ohio's Ancient American Indian Cultures.* Wilmington: Orange Frazer Press, 2005. 195.

[206] Jefferson, Thomas. "Query XI" in *The Portable Thomas Jefferson.* Merrill Peterson, ed., New York: Penguin Books, 1977, 141.

the Hamilton County State Line Site concur with Jefferson's two-century-old observations, discovering "projectile points embedded in only three of 390 burials."[207]

The civilizations of the Late Prehistoric Period are classified today as the "Fort Ancient" and "Missippian" cultures. In her 1998 report, titled *The Archaeological Reconnaissance of Ohio River Island National Wildlife Refuge*, Melissa Diamanti concluded

> The Fort Ancient and Mississippian cultural sequence can be described as a period of Mesoamerican-influenced cultural complexity built on a very effective subsistence base. Cahokia, a Mississippian center in Illinois, controlled a sphere of influence that extended into the middle Ohio River Valley.[208]

Both cultures built "hilltop forts accompanied by plaza complexes," writes Diamanti. There were ascribed tombs and sophisticated burial places. Archeology relies on the dead to tell about the living and discovering allocated places of the buried dead implies not just organization, but relative permanence. Hunters are buried in the field, heroes are buried in tombs.

Diamanti's work also uncovered shell-tempered pottery. This ceramic art differentiated the many tribes and expressed a sense of ethnic unity and identity. It was "decorated with a variety of regionally-distinctive incised and stamped

---

[207] Lepper, *Ohio Archeology.* 203.

[208] Diamanti, Melissa 1998. *Archaeological Reconnaissance of Ohio River Island National Wildlife Refuge in Pennsylvania, West Virginian and Kentucky and Phase I Archaeological Survey of Manchester Island No. 2, Kentucky*. Report submitted to the U. S. Fish and Wildlife Service, Region 5, Hadley, Ma.

patterns."[209] Diamanti discovered a peculiar pottery technique that employed riverine agents and local additives to prohibit shrinking and splitting in the firing process such as ground mussel shells or potsherds.[210]

Most all Fort Ancient sites' archeological excavations uncovered stockades and a geometric town structure and housing pattern centered around the pivotal town courtyard.[211] Findings suggest that these towns, as well as their citizens, observed strict, community-centric planning and government. Ohio's SunWatch village is a prime example. Modern archeological work suggests an agricultural and economic application to the greatly mysterious pole system bordering the central ceremonial area of the town. This concentric pattern— closely related in appearance, although not in magnitude, to the English monolithic structure, Stonehenge—was discovered to be a giant sun calendar, marking the planting and harvesting days of each year.[212] Lepper concluded

> Late Prehistoric villages were like almost any small community of farmers: everyone worked. The men likely cleared the fields and hunted game. The woman probably did the planting, weeding, harvesting, and grinding of the corn, while the children helped out and also watched the fields to keep of marauding crows and deer.[213]

---

[209] Lepper, *Ohio Archeology.* 198.
[210] "Museum of Native American Artifacts-MISSISSIPPIAN PERIOD 900 AD - 1450 AD". Retrieved 2010-07-18.
[211] Diamanti, *Archaeological Reconnaissance. No. 2.*
[212] Lepper, *Ohio Archeology.* 209.
[213] Lepper, *Ohio Archeology.* 203.

By the end of the fifteenth century, the cultural evolution of the Late Prehistoric Period culminated in many sedentary, permanent, and thriving settlements within the great Ohio River Valley.[214] They were a prehistoric people but not uncivilized; they were primordial yet highly dynamic.[215] Most importantly, they were a people developed by the millennia yet not a part of the millennia's developments, a natural people viewed as entirely unnatural on earth.

By the sixteenth century, modernity's incursion forever halted the civilizing evolutions of America's native cultures. Such invaders were cloaked as European explorers, settlers, and Christians. Native cultures had developed in an ancient vacuum and in a particular ecological niche. It is popularly concluded, moreover, that even before direct contact, European presence on the periphery unbalanced the ecological, geographical, and political systems that developed quietly over the millenniums. Stephen Aaron concluded that the depopulation of the Ohio Country began long before "Daniel Boone or any other Anglo-American hunters crossed the Appalachians."[216]

The Fur Trade Wars—also called the Beaver or Iroquois Wars (1630 AD – 1680 AD)—exemplify this causal relationship of indirect imbalance. Before New World contact, most European markets imported their furs from northern regions such as Scandinavia or Russia. The mid-sixteenth century saw the influx of New World goods, however, and the hungry European markets tasted the opulent, less-expensive,

---

[214] Johnson, W.C. 1981. *The Campbell Farm Site (36FA26) and Monongahela: A Preliminary Examination and Assessment*. Paper presented at the Fourth Monongahela Symposium, State College, Pennsylvania.
[215] It pains to write "prehistoric," due to the negativity implied therein. What I mean is prehistoric in that Europeans did not have their history.
[216] Aaron, *How the West Was Lost.* 7.

and higher quality American furs. Years before permanent European settlement, such furs were obtained from Basque fishermen off Newfoundland's Grand Banks and around the St. Lawrence River's estuary. The American beaver was the principle fur traded, due to its longevity, warmth, and luxurious texture. As European interest in these furs increased, so also increased the local tribe's desire for economic supremacy. A monopoly on the fur trade would not only supply advantageous funds to the tribal economy but also cement its standing as the most powerful among the many surrounding nations.

The Iroquois Nation—formed in about 1575 in central New York—greatly desired such a position. Known as the League of Five Nations, the Iroquois numbered between twenty and thirty thousand. Their adept warriors traded bounties of beavers for wool blankets, European muskets, iron tools, shirts, and ornamental beads. Early Ohio historian R. Douglas Hurt commented in his book, *The Ohio Frontier,* "Quickly, beaver became the first cash crop of North America and beaver skins the monetary medium of change." By mid-century, however, over-trapping decimated the Native's environment and destabilized their powerful position. By the late 1640s, most fur-bearing animals—especially the beaver—were nearly extinct in the Iroquois homeland.[217] Additionally, the Iroquois' interaction with European genomes and technology witnessed the devastating reduction of their populace. Endemic diseased pervaded their ranks and inoculable warfare plagued their tribe's balance.

To satisfy their voracious desires and repopulate their ranks, due to the "demographic and economic factors, closely

---

[217] Hurt, R. Douglas. *The Ohio Frontier: Crucible of the Old Northwest, 1720-1830.* Bloomington: Indiana University Press, 1996. 7.

tied to European colonialism," the Iroquois set their eyes on the rich hunting ground of the Ohio Country.[218] Pressured by their own undoing, this quest for control is known today as one of the bloodiest conflicts in North American history. The Iroquois— the Mohawk in particular—speedily destroyed many tribal confederacies of the Ohio Country, including the Tobacco, Neutral, Erie, Attiwandaron, Huron, Susquehannock, and Shawnee Nations, in order to gain control of its fertile valleys.[219] By 1654, the Iroquois dominated the "Ontario Peninsula," stretching from the Niagara River to the east of Lake Huron. Their ascendency, however, came at a price. The Iroquois disrupted age-old tribal geography from Lake Champlain to the Mississippi River and eradicated all sedentary settlements in their wake. The Shawnee in particular splintered into contingent populations that drifted to Alabama, Georgia, the Carolinas, and Pennsylvania.[220]

The power struggle created by European markets three thousand miles away indirectly raped the precious ecology of the Iroquois homeland and spread havoc across the Ohio Country, destroying its ten-thousand-year-old history before its veiled civilizations ever saw one white man. Perhaps, there is a natural clash between economics and nature, for the European notion of wealth—of labor and property—inculcated the Native

---

[218] Aaron, *How the West Was Lost.* 7.

[219] Richter, Daniel K. *The Ordeal of the Long-House: The Peoples of the Iroquois League in the Era of European Colonization* (Chapil Hill, 1992) 144-149; A. Gwynn Henderson, Cynthia E. Jobe, and Christopher A. Turnbow, *Indian Occupation and Use in Northern and Eastern Kentucky during the Contact Period (1540-1795): An Initial Investigation* (Frankfort, 1986).

[220] Callender, Charles, "Shawnee," in Bruce G. Trigger, ed., *Handbook of North American Indians,* 20 vols. (Washington, D., 1978), 15:630-634.

with savage proclivities and obliterated previously harmonious and peaceable instincts.

A Native History

In his 1830s examination of the Amerindians, George Catlin wrote a two-volume treaty detailing his many years spent among the Natives. He observed

> The Indians of North America ... are copper-coloured, with long black hair, black eyes, tall, straight, and elastic forms—are less than two millions in number—were originally the undisputed owners of the soil, and got their title to their lands from the Great Spirit who created them on it, were once a happy and flourishing people, enjoying all the comforts and luxuries of life which they knew of, and consequently cared for; were sixteen millions in numbers, and sent that number of daily prayers to the Almighty, and thanks for his goodness and protection.

Catlin continued

> Their country was entered by white men, but a few hundred years since; and thirty millions of these are now scuffling for the goods and luxuries of life, over the bones and ashes of twelve millions of red men; six millions of whom have fallen victims to the small-pox, and the remainder to the sword, the bayonet, and whiskey; all of which means of their death and destruction have been introduced and visited upon them by acquisitive white men; and by when men, also, whose forefathers were

welcomed and embraced in the land where the poor Indian met and fed them with 'ears of green corn and with pemican.'[221]

Catlin's account emphasized both the genetic and physical results of European contact. Directly or indirectly, Native civilization's progress perished under the biological and physical European gun. Although both routes led to the same end—near-complete devastation—individual analysis is required for each individual germ.

This "catastrophic" and inadvertent biological gun, writes modern historian William McNeill in his 1976 book, *Plagues and Peoples*, resulted in one of the greatest "population decay[s]" of the modern era.[222] Modern scholarship surprisingly agrees with Catlin's early-nineteenth-century estimate. It is believed that perhaps more than ten million people inhabited the region north of the Rio Grande by the turn of the sixteenth century—more than double the number that inhabited the British Isles during the same period.[223] Catlin's observations, although racist in their own ways, speak to the truth behind the depopulation of Colonial America. Select modern estimates conclude that Native culture before contact could have exceeded seventy million people. In either case, David Cook of the University of Texas at Austin concluded that the depopulation of the Native peoples in the first century as a result of contact with European colonists was undeniably the "greatest human

[221] Catlin, George, *Letters and Notes on the Manners, Customs, and Conditions of the North American Indians*. New York: Dover Publications, Inc., 1973. 6.

[222] McNeill, William H, *Plagues and Peoples.* Garden City: Anchor Press, 1976.

[223] Lord, Lewis. "How Many People Were Here Before Columbus?" in *The U.S. News & World Report*, 1997, pp. 68-70.

catastrophe in history, far exceeding even the disaster of the Black Death of medieval Europe."[224]

Native populations in some areas were reduced by ninety to ninety-five percent, losing millions to disease in only a few decades.[225] Entire towns witnessed the speedy decay of their populace, mothers burying their children one at a time. The most devastating diseases were smallpox, typhus, measles, influenza, bubonic plague, cholera, malaria, tuberculosis, mumps, yellow fever, and pertussis.[226]

The physical gun was no more obvious than its biological counterpart. Both European weaponry and their physical presence within the New World greatly disrupted the balance of the Old. Between the French's initial permeation of the Ohio River Valley in the mid-to-late seventeenth century and John Findley's entrance into its great southern valley a hundred years later, the Native's habitual presence in the region was dismantled and their hamlets and villages almost entirely dissipated.

The eastern bluegrass Chaouanon town of Eskippathiki serves as a great example. In a 1734 French census, the sedentary Shawnee settlement boasted two hundred men. In Findley and Boone's 1769 journey to the region—just thirty-five years later—the village was entirely gone. In 1750, the Delaware chief "King Beaver" sensed the danger on the horizon

---

[224] Cook, Noble David. *Born To Die*. Cambridge: Cambridge University Press, 1998; pp. 1-14.
[225] Miller, Randall M., Pencak, William A., eds. *Pennsylvania: A History of the Commonwealth*. Penn State University Press; 1 edition (October 22, 2002), 35.
[226] Aberth, John. *The First Horseman: Disease in Human History*. Pearson-Prentice Hall, 2007. 51.

and prophesied, "A high Wind is rising." Little did he know how quickly his divine foresight would come to fruition.

Interminable episodes of European pressure—such as the Fur Trade Wars—continually pushed the Natives of the Ohio Country westward and forced them to adapt migratory and nomadic proclivities. The resulting bareness of their wake's region was ironically complimented by its reputation as a supreme hunting ground, boasting garden-like abundance. One hundred years after the Fur Trade Wars, in 1750, Dr. Thomas Walker was sent by the Loyal Company of Virginia to observe and reconnoiter the western slopes of the Appalachians. Overwhelmed by his findings, he wrote in his journal, "We killed in the Journey 13 Buffaloes, 8 Elks, 53 Bear, 20 Deer, 4 Wild Geese, about 150 Turkeys, besides small game." He continued, "We might have killed three times as much meat, if we had wanted it."[227] Another hunter boasted the same luxuriance, "Turkeys so numerous it might be said they appeared but one flock, universally scattered in the woods."[228] Absent from such records were any reports of civilizations or settled peoples.

Such rich accounts of wildlife do not explain the origin of this great hunting ground, nor do they tell of the Natives that once hunted and shaped the abundantly fruitful ecology. The Ohio Country of the eighteenth and nineteenth centuries was strategically hunted, but not inhabited by Native Americans. The absence of human permanence fostered a land rich in natural guilds and with great diversity; a land of supreme irony: one begging to be hunted and settled but filled by only hunter-

---

[227] Johnson, J. Stoddard. ed., *First Explorations of Kentucky: Journals of Dr. Thomas Walker, 1750, and Christopher Gist, 1751* (Louisville, 1898), 75.
[228] Draper, Lyman. "Sketches from Border Life," Draper MSS, 27CC33;

gatherers. Stephen Aaron summarized such irony, writing, "Why Indians hunted but did not reside in the region puzzled European attestants, who knew little of the history and culture of the Indian peoples of the Ohio Valley."[229] The presence of Europeans dismantled Native communities centuries before, forming vacuums of regional power and geographic position.

Based on archeological, historical, and anthropological evidence, it is clear that there was culture before contact.[230] However, the mind of European history could only stretch so far as its eyes could see, and the contact was all it saw. In their bloated and blindly racist assumptions, European explorers dismissed the import of Native cultures and their magnificent monuments, ascribing their constructions to one of the lost tribes of Israel, Greeks, Vikings, Hindus, or Phoenicians.

A prime example is found in Query XI of Thomas Jefferson's *Notes on the State of Virginia,* wherein Jefferson refused to acknowledge any Native monuments in America. He wrote, "I know of no such thing existing as an Indian monument," and, he continued, "Of labour on the large scale, I think there is no remain as respectable as would be a common ditch for the draining of lands."[231] In an anonymous 1775 letter to the *Royal American Magazine* of Boston, a prehistoric earthwork in the Ohio County was drawn and described. However, nowhere in its voluminous description of the mound's great plan did the author attribute the local and savage Native as its civilized authors.[232] Although Native monuments were

---

[229] Aaron, *How the West Was Lost.* 6.

[230] The phrase, "culture before contact" is taken from the title of the publication, "Cultures Before Contact: The Late Prehistory of Ohio and Surrounding Regions," edited by Robert A Genheimer.

[231] Jefferson, Thomas Jefferson, "Query XI" in *The Portable Thomas Jefferson.*

[232] Lepper, *Ohio Archeology.* 238.

rivaled by those hailed in Central and Eastern Europe as "Wonders of the World," their creators—generations of cultured individuals, engineers, and architects—were forever discarded and labeled as savages, unfit and unequal for consideration.

These rich civilizations perished without a written history and their people were forgotten with only little remorse. Thomas Jefferson may have lamented the fact that "we have suffered so many of the Indian tribes already to extinguish" but it was only because he had not "previously collected...the rudiments at least" of their languages.[233] The loss of possible scientific research was all Jefferson mourned.

In his 1835 examination of American Democracy, Alexis de Tocqueville observed that the Native had but two "options for salvation: war or civilization." He declared that "civilization is the result of a long social endeavor that operates in one same place, and that different generations hand down."[234] Therefore, he concluded, the nomadic Native was a barbarian in the true sense: not Greek, not Western, and certainly not civilized. What Tocqueville appeared to neglect, however, was that it was the biological and literal war inherent to European colonization that uprooted ten-thousand-year-old civilizations and greatly attributed to the de-civilization of the Native American. Tocqueville's examination also missed the mark, as it was aimed at the wrong target. He searched for a civilization like his, applying only one set of rules and definitions.

In the most basic form, Tocqueville's cure was the germ. It was Western civilization that eradicated the civilization of the West. Although Tocqueville did not question the Native's

---

[233] Jefferson, *Query XI*. 143.
[234] Tocqueville, *Democracy in America*. *312*-313.

ability to become civilized under the strictly European definition, he misplaced their motive and misunderstood their history.

Pride

The American Native was motivated by an age-old pride. In his Pulitzer Prize-winning book, *American Heroes, Profiles of Men and Women Who Shapes Early America,* historian Edmund S. Morgan writes that the "unyielding Indian" should greatly "impress" anyone "who reads vary far in [their] voluminous literature." Morgan wrote of the Native's uniqueness and boasted of their "overwhelming diversity." He concluded that "linguists today recognize 375 different languages" among the many Native nations.[235] Tocqueville himself recognized such supreme diversity and pride. In volume one of his *Democracy in America,* Tocqueville concluded, "The Indian...lives and dies in the midst of these dreams of his pride." He asserted

> To the perfection of our arts he wants to oppose only the resources of the wilderness; to our tactics, only his undisciplined courage; to the profundity of our design, only the spontaneous instincts of his savage nature. He succumbs in this unequal struggle.[236]

For Tocqueville, however, the Amerindians' yearning for the utmost "freedom of the woods" was driven by their pride against

[235] Morgan, Edmund S. *American Heroes: Profiles of Men and Women who Shaped Early America.* New York: W.W. Norton & Company, 2010., 39; 41.
[236] Tocqueville, *Democracy in America.* 305-306.

European definitions of civilization. Although not altogether untrue, the Native's true pride was driven by something much deeper—a pride for the civilization of their past. Enrique Salmon, an indigenous ethnobotanist attributed this pride to what he termed "cultural history." Salmon writes, "it's a way of perceiving ourselves as part of an extended ecological family of all species." A connection that "shares ancestry, origins, and breath" and is only viable "when we view the life surrounding us as family." The Native's pride was for connection and shared breath.[237]

Edmond Morgan summarized this subtle conflict as a clash between distant worlds

> In Europe, and indeed in most of the world, the acquisition and possession of riches constitutes the ultimate basis for social esteem. We may think it better to be born rich than to become rich, but in our society wealth has seldom been thought a handicap. Among the Indians, on the other hand, there existed a deliberate indifference to wealth, and indifference that could sometimes be infuriating to the white man. …The Indian could afford to scorn riches and to shun the industry necessary to acquire them, because in his society it was the man that counted, not what he owned.[238]

The many observations and treatises of the Native Americans' political, religious, and social life during the late

---

[237] Salmon, Enrique, "Sharing Breath" in *Colors of Nature: Culture Identity, and the Natural World.* Alison H Deming & Lauret E Savoy, ed., Minneapolis: Milweek Editions, 2011. 197.

[238] Morgan, *American Heroes.* 50.

Colonial period speak to this pride's deep permeation into tribal ecology. In the spring of 1755, Colonel James Smith was captured by the Delaware Indians while pioneering Braddock's Road, a "12-foot highway through the Virginian forest"[239] For the next four years, Smith lived and hunted with his captives, learning much of their ways and experiencing many of their customs. Although his subsequent narrative speaks bountifully of the Delaware Indians' habits and customs, Smith's philosophical observations of his Native captors provide a unique insight into their pride for their civilization.

Two years into his "captivity," Smith hunted along the Ollentangy River with his new stepbrother and Delaware chief, Tecaughretanego, who he described as "an eminent counselor," a "first-rate warrior, statesman, and hunter," and "a truly great man."[240] Nearly fifty years later, Smith, who later served as a delegate in the American Continental Congress, signed the American Declaration of Independence, and served in the Kentucky Legislature, furthered his praise of his brother, writing

> Tecaughretanego was no common person, but was among the Indians as Socrates in the ancient heathen world; and, it may be, equal to him, if not in wisdom and in learning, yet perhaps in patience and fortitude.[241]

---

239 Lewis, Jon E. *The Mammoth Book of The West.* 16.
240 Smith, James. "Col. James Smith's Life Among the Delawares, 1755-1759" in *The Account of Mary Rowlandson and Other Indian Captivity Narratives.* Horace Kephart, ed. Mineola: Dover Publications, 1915. 31; 35; 38.
241 Smith, James. *The Account of Mary Rowlandson.* 38.

The most striking aspect of his remembrances is their irony. Hidden in his words is a subtle critique of the foundation of Western civilization. Smith, the champion revolutionary leader and lawyer, rebuked his civilization's founder and praised the savages of the wilderness. He compared the Native's civilization with that of ancient Greece, but dubbed only the latter as "heathen." Smith argued that the only difference between Tecaughretanego and Socrates was in their opportunity to acquire knowledge, or "learning." Smith claimed that, although Tecaughretanego may not be equal "in wisdom and in learning," his stepbrother surpassed Socrates in "patience and fortitude." These latter philosophic qualities are seemingly more important to the highly educated and intellectual Smith.

Upon one occasion, Smith was intimated with the Delaware Indians' policy of community and honor. While camped near the falls of Canesadooharie (what is today either the Huron River or the Black River of Lorain County), Tontileaugo left Smith to go on a day's hunt. While Smith was at camp alone, a Wyandot warrior visited and Smith supplied the famished guest with a "shoulder of venison" and then he departed. Upon his return to camp and learning of such action, however, Tontileaugo accused Smith of "behaving just like a Dutchman."[242] Continuing his admonishment, Tontileaugo questioned

> "Do you not know that when strangers come to our camp we ought always to give them the best we have?...[you]

---

[242] The Dutch he called Skoharehaugo, which took its derivation from a Dutch settlement called Skoharey.

must learn to behave like a warrior, and do great things, and never be found in any such little actions."[243]

The Christian and Pennsylvania-raised Smith was shocked. Tontileaugo would have starved himself to feed the stranger—who here is the barbarian and who is the civilized? Smith later wrote that, along with their giving spirit

> It is seldom that Indians do steal anything from one another. And they say that they never did, until the white people came among them, and taught some of them to lie, cheat, and steal.

During the four years with his stepbrother, Smith grew to understand the natural philosophy of the Native. Although their "learning" of the wilderness was great and their abilities within its wooded blockade magnificent, Native philosophy centered on thankfulness, fortitude, and the human heart. Smith remembered that, over a sumptuous feast of roasted Buffalo, Tecaughretanego blessed the food and talked of the "necessity and pleasure of receiving the necessary supports of life with thankfulness," as Owaneeyo is the "great giver."[244]

The Native's pride was also centered on human dignity. "The whole Indian mode of government was designed to emphasize" the inherent "dignity of the individual," wrote Edmund Morgan.[245] In his 1765 treatise, *A Concise Account of*

---

[243] Smith, James. *The Account of Mary Rowlandson.* 18.

[244] Owaneeyo is roughply translated to "God" or "Creator." Source: Smith, James. *The Account of Mary Rowlandson.* 38.

[245] Morgan, *American Heroes.* 50.

North America, the innovative and exemplar commander of the French and Indian War Robert Rogers documented

> The great and fundamental principles of [the Indian's] policy are, that every man is naturally free and independent; that no one...on earth has any right to deprive him of his freedom and independency, and that nothing can be compensation for the loss of it.

This clear, backwoods, and free account of the natural rights of man was written ten years before the white man's Declaration of Independence and described not Western civilization's enlightened mind but the free mind of the civilized West. Cadwallader Colden, the early-eighteenth-century physician, natural scientist, and lieutenant governor of New York wrote similarly of the Iroquois Nation. In his 1727 book, *The History of the Five Indian Nations of Canada,* he asserted

> Each Nation is an absolute Republick by its self, govern'd in all Publick Affairs of War and Peace by the Sachems or Old Men, who Authority and Power is gain'd by and consists wholly in the Opinion the rest of the Nation have of their Wisdom and Integrity. They never execute their Resolutions by Compulsion or Force upon any of their People.[246]

Colden's observation of republican government among the Iroquois predated those of the American Founding Fathers by

---

[246] Colden, Cadwallader. *The History of the Five Indian Nations of Canada,* 1727.

over sixty years. In 1787, American Founding Father Alexander Hamilton introduced *The Federalist*, arguing that it has been "reserved to the people of this country to decide" whether "good government" can be formed by "reflection and choice," or, if the world is "forever destined to depend...on accident and force." Hamilton was correct when he argued that it was up to "the people of this country" to decide and prove a shining example to the world. What he did not know, however, was that the principles of independence, equality, the natural rights of man, and the practices of republican government were already firmly established and brightly shining. They were not new inventions on the American shores. Moreover, it was the budding American regime that, by accident, forced the age-old reflections of republicanism and natural right into oblivion.

Lt. Henry Timberlake's 1765 *Memoirs* also provides strikingly vivid details about how the Native American's pride is depicted in their philosophy and modes of government. Timberlake spent over three months living amongst the Cherokee Indians of the Overhill country in early 1762—the same Indians Daniel Boone became highly acquainted with ten years later. Timberlake's observations depict an ordered, agricultural, and natural civilization. The Cherokee people, he wrote, are of a "good uncultivated genius" and are "fond of speaking well." Their government was honest and was some form of a republic. He wrote, "Merit alone creates their minister, and not the prejudice of party, which often creates ours."[247] When Timberlake compared the Cherokee's government to

---

[247] Timberlake, Henry. *The Memoirs of Lt. Henry Timberlake: The Story of a Soldier, Adventurer, and Emissary to the Cherokees, 1756-1765*. Duane H. King, ed., Cherokee: Cherokee Indian Press, 2007. *30; 36-37*.

"ours," he praised the former and rebuked the latter—the great political institution of England.

Timberlake's ethnographical observations also took into account the health of the Cherokee people. In a time when the average life-expectancy of a European was thirty-five years, Timberlake wrote that a woman in the Cherokee village

> …still continues her laborious tasks, and has yet strength enough to carry two hundred weight of wood on her back near a couple of miles. I am apt to think some of them, by their own computation, are near one hundred and fifty years old.

Timberlake was not the only European observer to make note of the supreme health of the American Native. In the 1830s, George Catlin spent six years documenting and painting over fifty different Native tribes. Among his research, Catlin noted that the teeth of the Crow and Osage were "as regular as the keys of a piano." In addition, he never met anyone who was ever ill, sick, or deformed.

Catlin observed that the "great secret of life" was breathing. The Natives argued that "breath inhaled through the mouth sapped the body of strength, deformed the face, and caused stress and disease." They instead practiced nose breathing, an exercise that "kept the body strong, made the face beautiful, and prevented disease."[248] If the progress of civilization is the cure to the state of nature, of ill-health, then why did George Washington's teeth fall out and why was the

---

[248] Nestor, James. *Breath, The New Science of a Lost Art.* New York: Riverhead Books, 2020. 46-47.

leading cause of death among white civilization during this period dysentery—a disease caused by poor hygiene and poor foods?[249]

Regardless of Catlin's and Timberlake's shared focus on the health of the Native, Timberlake's work is elusive and his depictions circumspect, providing enough information to momentarily pique the reader's thirst while leaving them forever desiring more. The subtle nature of his work may be the most telling depiction of the Cherokee people: they are a mysteriously guarded but judicious people, driven forever to their past while standing on the periphery of the future.

A self-described "English Chikkasah," James Adair observed similar traits among the Natives living between Georgia and Virginia. His voluminous 1775 account *The History of the American Indians* is today regarded as "one of the most valuable primary accounts of the Southeastern Indians."[250] Adair perceived that the Natives were

> Governed by the plain and honest law of nature, their whole constitution breathes nothing but liberty: and, when there is that equality of conditions, manners, and privileges, and a constant familiarity in society, as prevails in every Indian nation, and through all our British colonies, there glows such a chearfulness and warmth of courage in each of their breasts, as cannot be described.[251]

---

[249] University of Gothenburg. "Dysentery epidemic killed many in the 1700s-1800s." ScienceDaily. ScienceDaily, 25 October 2012.

[250] Adair, James. *The History of the American Indians*. Kathryn E. Holland Braund, ed., Tuscaloosa: The University of Alabama Press, 2005. xi.
[251] Adair, James. *The History of the American Indians*. 375.

Although "it is reputed merit alone" that drove their social and political communities, Adair claimed that the Natives took great care in providing for their poor and for crafting "wisely framed" and honest laws. Mid-nineteenth-century American author James Fenimore Cooper argued in his notable work, *The Pioneers,* that law is what separates the civilized from the savage. Adair concludes his work asserting that his keen and extended observation of the Southeastern Natives produced a portrait antithetical to the popular image of the Native American as the "savage of the wilderness."

He delivered them as courageous yet meek, cunning yet honest. Most importantly, Adair observed a civilization driven by virtue and formed by laws. He concluded that the Native system ultimately accorded with the "grand fundamental law— 'A natural ex, a virtue rex'"—meaning 'Law by Nature, King by Virtue.'[252] In Ancient Greece, "barbarians" were those who were simply non-Greek. Strikingly, Adair concluded his voluminous work with the most famous of the Greek's— Alexander the Great's—last words to describe those whom his society had rejected as barbarians—"A natural ex, a virtue rex."

The American Native was both a challenge and an insult to their European neighbors. In his book *Sand Talk: How Indigenous Thinking Can Save the World,* Tyson Yunkaporta argued that "civilizations are cultures that create cities, communities that consume everything around them," and then, ultimately, they consume "themselves."[253] The American Native was the perfection of Europe's virtues mixed with the

---

[252] Adair, *The History of the American Indians.* 416-421; 422.
[253] Yunkaporta, Tyson. *Sand Talk: How Indigenous Thinking Can Save the World.* New York: HarperOne, 2020. 49-50.

failures of its worldly vices. They had the virtues of culture without the vices of civilization.

Their pride yielded extreme actions of compassion and cruelty, of chastity and courage. Their lives danced with the rhythms of the seasons yet their song was quieter than the morning dew. They were expressive yet said little, philosophical yet proud of being as thoughtless as the birds. Perhaps it was these inherent ironies masked by the veil of the natural world that forever tainted the Europeans' impressions of the Native American. We must learn to see.

A New Education

If the Anglo-Native collision produced negative effects for the latter, it was overall advantageous for the former. Although hailed as pioneers, most European immigrants knew nothing of the hunt, weaponry, or subsisting within raw nature. Daniel Boone's ancestors were Quakers from Southern England with little skill or knowledge in handling weaponry or navigating the woods. They were farmers and weavers as well as plowmen and homesteaders. Historically, Europeans were prohibited from participating in the hunt and every western movement they made plainly proved their naturally resulting inefficacy. Learning to hunt was one of the many adjustments these backcountry Pennsylvanian pioneers made—and made quickly. Stephen Aaron noted, "While the peoples of the backcountry imported a variety of subsistence traditions, all faced a seasoning period in which old ways were adapted to new conditions."

New conditions required a new education. Faced by the rugged and wholly untamed frontier, the settlers' education was both on the technical and on the technique. Aaron wrote, "Technology obviously mattered to hunters, but technique counted more."[254] Early nineteenth century Boone historian John Mason Peck summarized both the character and importance of this education. He wrote

> To gain the skill of an accomplished hunter requires talents, patience, perseverance, sagacity, and habits of thinking. Amongst other qualifications, knowledge of human nature, and especially of Indian character, is indispensable to the pioneer of the wilderness. Add to these, self-possession, self-control, and promptness in execution. Persons who are unaccustomed to a frontier residence know not how much, in the preservation of life, and in obtaining subsistence, depends on such characteristics.[255]

The characteristics of the hunt required a natural mastery of oneself and his surroundings.

To be able to shoot was good but to be able to harvest was better. On the hunt, the technical sharpshooter was always surpassed by the technique of the hunter. To locate was better than to mark and to harvest wisely was best of all. Take for example the Kentucky buffalo hunt. In the mid-eighteenth century, the volume and density of the Kentucky herd was so concentrated that it seemed a hunter's meal was as good as his aim.

The educated hunter knew better. In his early-nineteenth-century interview with Reverend John D. Shane,

---

[254] Aaron, *How the West Was Lost.* 21-22.
[255] Peck, *Life of Daniel Boone.* 5.

western pioneer William Clinkenbeard emphasized his technique. He believed, "Kill the leader if you could find it out, and you might kill three or four [buffalos]."[256] This was because buffalo are a mob stocking and herding animal. Fall the leader, the rest of the herd will roam directionless, supplying the hunter ample time to reload and increase his bounty. Pioneer Abraham Thomas wrote that during one hunt he employed such a measure and "had we been disposed, we might have shot the whole gang."[257]

The late-eighteenth-century frontiersman Michael Stoner also serves as a great example. He was often described as being "an indifferent hand to shoot at mark...but at game, he was the best man in Kentucky." Stoner prospered on the frontier because he understood the technique, even if not the technology—he "seemed to understand the motions of living animals" better than the releasing mechanism of his flintlock.[258] Stephen Aaron concluded, "A solid education in animal habits and habitats means the difference between success and very serious failure."[259] Such an education was lost on most early hunters. Standing on the herd's windward side, they would fall the wrong buffalo first. This blunder not only reduced their harvest of fresh meat and animal hide but it also created a stampede in their direction. Every pioneer, hunter, frontiersman, and settler faced the harsh reality of the New World's entirely new education.

---

[256] Lucien Beckner, ed., "Reverend John D. Shane's Interview with Pioneer William Clinkenbeard," *FCHQ* 2 (April 1928): 106.
[257] Clough, Elizabeth Thatcher, ed., "Abraham Thomas: 'This Small Legacy of Experience'," *Kentucky Ancestors 26* (Autumn 1990): 77.
[258] Enoch, Harry G. *Pioneer Voices: Interviews with Early Settlers of Clark County Kentucky.* 128.
[259] Aaron, *How the West Was Lost.* 23.

120

In his chilling novel, *The Revenant,* Michael Punke writes of the frontier as a fierce teacher of "collective responsibility." He concluded, "Though no law was written, there was a crude rule of law, adherence to a covenant that transcended...selfish interests."[260] Since the natural world of the frontier required a firm dedication to acquiring this new education, pioneers were lucky that it also supplied the means—the experienced Native.

In Europe, hunting was a sport, regulated by the government and solely patronized by aristocrats. In the arduous and severe lands of the American backcountry, however, hunting was a necessity, regulated by the laws of nature and included the ranks of only the strongest and most-rugged souls. Every step westward was a step away from the lives of their ancestors and toward Native ways. Although extreme, the shift was gradual. Obtaining an intimate acquaintance with nature and its subtle movements required tutelage and time.

In his late-eighteenth-century work, *Notes on the Settlement and Indian Wars of the Western Parts of Virginia and Pennsylvania,* Joseph Doddridge concluded that European settlers acquired this tutelage—"how to dress, how to track, how to decoy, how to wait patiently and silently, how to live off the land"—directly from their observations of and associations with the Native.[261]

The practical use of European technology, combined with the important fundamentals of Native technique, transformed the pioneer's mode of subsistence to abundance

---

[260] Punke, Michael. *The Revenant.* New York: Picador Publishing, 2002. 39.
[261] Joseph Doddridge, *Notes on the Settlement and Indian Wars of the Western Parts of Virginia and Pennsylvania from 1763-1783 inclusive, Together with a Review of the State of Society and Manners of the First Settlers of the Western Country.* Pittsburgh, 1824. 179. 83.

and transfigured their enlightened philosophy to a magical romance. This blending showed that the woods of the American West were animated, acted on by magical powers, yet subject to the hunter's iron will. For the Native, the hunt was a sacred act of spirituality, for they had a deep and ancient kinship with animals and the natural world. For the white man, the hunt was an almost sacred act of mastery—of manhood and of self-inflated dominion. In general, most European settlers benefited under the tutelage of the "how of the wilderness" but few stooped to learn the ever important "why." Today, are we any different?

CHAPTER 6

Threading the Needle

The Woods of My Youth

Daniel Boone was an early pupil of the wilderness. The woods of his youth teemed with more than wildlife—it teemed with life. The early-eighteenth-century Quaker homestead observed many peculiar shadows within its wooded periphery, welcomed its many whispers, and befriended its multitude of mysterious movements. The illimitable forests of the Pennsylvanian frontier illuminated Daniel's youthful restlessness and curiosity. In the boundless freedom of her woods he found peace, and under her quiet canopy her found consolation and the great expression of his soul. Robert Morgan noted, "For Daniel, the forest was his mother's world, a place of shadows and mystery, infinite diversions and pleasures."[262] Beyond this enchantment, however, it was also his teacher. The story of Daniel's westward movement is a story of his ever-heightening appreciation of the natural world and its many natural civilizations.

The Boone homestead was familiar with its native neighbors. In 1728, six years before Daniel was born, Native

---

[262] Morgan, *Boone: A Biography.* 10.

relations in the region intensified. Anticipating a raid, most inhabitants of the Bucks County frontier "generally fled" for the safety of surrounding towns. Obstinately, however, the Justice of the Peace sent a dispatch to the colonial governor pleading for support "in order to defend our fronteers." He continued

> There remains about twenty men with me to guard my mill, where I have about 1000 bushels of wheat and fflour; and we are resolved to defend ourselves to ye last Extremity.[263]

Such a resolute and determined spirit was found in George Boone, Daniel's grandfather. Although often described as a family of careful and judicious Quakers, the Boones were fearless and tough, ready to "defend their possessions and rights with their lives."[264] They were of a hard stock, but maintained a gentle spirit.

During what is believed to be the same 1728 conflict, George Boone led the successful rescue effort of two Native women who were being held by a faction of white settlers, entertaining "lustful and murderous intentions."[265] This single 1728 episode lucidly portrays the ideology of the Boones. They seemed to always defend their own: if was their belief, their crop, their frontier, or their view of justice under attack. They were forever fighting and leading the charge.

By the time of Daniel's birth in 1734, Native relations had mostly settled.[266] In 1736, a party of Delaware led by

---

[263] Bakeless, *Daniel Boone.* 8.
[264] Lofaro, *Daniel Boone.* 6-7.
[265] Faragher, *Daniel Boone.* 19.
[266] Bakeless, *Daniel Boone.* 8.

Sassoonan—or Allummoppees[267], the "king" of the Schuylkill—visited George Boone, who now "enjoyed a reputation among the Indians for befriending natives."[268] The Delaware of the mid-eighteenth century were peaceful but not friendly with their white neighbors. They were not in the habit of visiting white settlements for community or rest. Boone Historian John Mack Faragher noted in his biography that such a visit was, therefore, "important enough to record" in the Provincial Records of Pennsylvania.[269] The Delaware's interest in the Boones was something extraordinary in the true sense of the word. They had not come to trade, barter, or engage in diplomacy. Rather, Sassoonan and his fellow braves emerged from the safety of their woods in search of Boone's trusted community.

On one occasion, the Quakers of Bucks County were alarmed by the arrival of a party of braves, dressed and painted for war. Expecting the worst, they readied for battle. To their surprise and great relief, however, they quickly learned that the Natives had come to their aid, believing that their "peaceful white brothers were in danger" from a neighboring tribe. Perhaps, such peaceful relations were due to the Quaker influence. Or perhaps, such relations were dependent upon the amiability and strong character of the Boone family, respected by the strong Native brave for their honor in life, charity, and courage under distress.

Daniel Boone was born into this world, but he also made it his own. In the introductory chapter of his book, *Daniel*

---

[267] In 1715 Sassoonana, also known as Allummoppees, succeeded his father Tamanend as Delaware chieftain of the Turtle Clan and maintained semi-friendly relations with English settlers until his death in the Autumn of 1747.

[268] Faragher, *Daniel Boone.* 19.

[269] Faragher, *Daniel Boone.* 19; Draper, *The Life of Daniel Boone.* 110.

Boone: Master of the Wilderness, John Bakeless wrote that Daniel's "fascination which the wilderness exercised on [him] to the end of his life began almost as early as his knowledge of Indians."[270] Daniel's youth in Penn's woods forever impressed upon him a love of the wilderness and an intimate connection with its natural inhabitants. Bakeless continued

> From these friendly aborigines [of his youth] the future Indian fighter was learning the red man's habits, character, and way of life, mastering the kinks and quirks of red psychology, gaining that amazing ability to 'think Indian' which in after life enabled him, when trailing Indians, to know exactly what they were going to do next. Many a pioneer document from the desperate and bloody Kentucky years shows Daniel Boone quietly assuring his companions that the Indians would soon do thus-and-so—as invariably they did![271]

The composite border region of Daniel's youth early afforded his restless and curious mind interesting subjects to experience and observe. Just as William Penn told the Delaware in early 1681 that he desired to "winn and gain their love and friendship by a kind, just and peaceable life," Daniel's youth in Penn's woods taught him the strength and honor of the magnanimous Native and impressed upon him a desire to live peacefully by their side.[272] Such natural scholarship instilled a "fervid love of

---

[270] Bakeless, *Daniel Boone.* 8-9.
[271] Bakeless, *Daniel Boone.* 9.
[272] Penn, William. Letter to the "King of the Indians," October 18, 1681, Richard Dunn and Mary Maples Dunn, eds., *The Papers of William Penn,* 5 vols. (Philadelphia: University of Pennsylvania Press, 1981-86), 2:128-129.

nature" and its exotic inhabitants within his impressionable mind.[273]

Early Meetings of Hunters

From the beginning, Daniel's calling to the woods was almost biblical in proportion. As a youth, Daniel's job was to follow the family cattle in the woods, returning them every evening for milking and for the protection of the immediate Boone homestead. One evening, during the mid 1740s, he became so absorbed in his own wooded expeditions that he overlooked the hour, his family, and his duties as herdsman and disappeared into the night. Although dusk, his mother's eyes could catch neither signs of the family herd nor the family herdsman returning for the night. Her characteristically cheerful disposition grew increasingly pessimistic.

Before she lost her cattle to the darkness—and to the Pennsylvanian frontier—the determined Welsh mother set out to make the five-mile trip to the family's pastures and round up the cattle herself. An adept frontierswoman, Sarah succeeded at her task and stayed her mind by milking, straining, and churning butter from the clabbered milk through the night. As the milk thickened and soured, however, so did the morning air. But Daniel was still not to be found. Calm but expecting the worst, Sarah made the trip back to town to get help.

The search party hunted from the Oley Hills to the Neversink Mountains—nine miles to the northwest—but found no traces of the young woodsman. The next morning the party determined to search even further into the Pennsylvanian

---

[273] Draper, *The Life of Daniel Boone.* 112.

wilderness. By evening, they spotted a column of smoke in the distance. Approaching slowly, as such an omen could lead to either hostility or promise, they found their hunter contently seated in "his temple," smoking a bearskin and roasting fresh meat. Looking up to find the search party's eyes furiously reflecting his fire's glare, Daniel calmly responded that he had started tracking the bear two days prior and did not want to waste it. Besides, the town got fresh bear meat and he an outlet for his restless spirit.

Although this story may not be historically true, as it appears only in later accounts of Boone's life, it reveals much about his character. A parallel to Luke's gospel account of the twelve-year-old Jesus lost from Mary and Joseph, but at home conversing in his "father's house," this story presents the twelve-year-old Daniel lost from the homestead but at home in nature's temple. Robert Morgan provided a simple anecdote for Daniel's natural calling: when he and his cronies played "Hunt the Indian," Daniel played the Indian and most often could not be found.[274]

The rugged experiences and inhabitants of the border taught Daniel the inimitable lessons of the hunt and the secret habits of wild animals. His youth was imbued with the allure of the woods, and its natives were his tutor. John Mack Faragher writes

> When [Daniel] ventured out of his own neighborhood into the woods surrounding the Schuylkill settlements, the young hunter entered a mixed cultural world. On woodland thoroughfares the hunters of many nations met,

---

[274] Morgan, *Boone: A Biography.* 16.

and over a smoke of tobacco or kinnikinnick, a pungent mixture of dried bark and leaves, they traded news and information.[275]

Daniel learned wilderness subsistence and survival early from his observations and many interactions with the Natives—how to find and apply the many medicinal roots, herbs, and wild berries of the forest, and how to adeptly track the movements of animals and mark the lay of the land. Most importantly, the curious youth learned of the many westward flowing rivers and heard many fireside tales of the Eden of the West.

The Boone family's move to the Yadkin Valley provided their young hunter an updated canvas for his passions. The Yadkin was a rougher and wilder country than Penn's woods. By the mid-eighteenth century, North Carolina had only twenty-five thousand inhabitants and its extreme western borderland of the Yadkin Valley contained much less. Lyman Draper described Daniel's revised woods as a "land of plenty and happiness."[276] The Boones settled in the undulating prairie north of the Yakin's forks known as Buffalo Lick. The land teamed with wildlife due to its rich canebrakes and luxurious meadows. John Bakeless boasted of the Yadkin's fertility, claiming that, in the beginning, a hunter could "take thirty deer a day without leaving the valley."[277]

In his late-twentieth-century account of the *Peopling of British North America,* Harvard Professor and Pulitzer Prize Winner Bernard Bailyn writes that, as early as 1700, the valley

---

[275] Faragher, *Daniel Boone.* 19.
[276] Draper, *The Life of Daniel Boone.* 126.
[277] Bakeless, *Daniel Boone.* 19.

exported fifty-four thousand deerskins to European markets.[278]
The colony's deerskin bounty was so opulent that a "buck"—"a
dressed skin weighing about two and a half pounds, worth about
forty cents a pound," or about a dollar per skin—became
synonymous for the American dollar.[279]

Hitherto, the hunt supplied Daniel an outlet for his
passions and recreation for his soul. In the sumptuous Yadkin
Valley, however, he could "unite profit with pleasure."[280] By
1753, Daniel's skills as a marksman, hunter, and scout were
wildly celebrated and honored. He supplied the local markets of
Salisbury with pelts, furs, and produce, profiting several
shillings for every bearskin or deer hide. Daniel also traded bear
bacon and ginseng for more traps, lead, and powder. Folklore
has it that Bear Creek in the Yadkin Valley was so named after
Daniel took ninety-one bears along its banks in one season.[281] A
winter trapper, Daniel left the woods in March with more profit
than a blacksmith or weaver could make in four years.

By his late teens, Daniel's ability to mark surpassed
even his Native neighbors. After depositing his furs in Salisbury
in the spring, he often partook in local shooting matches. Such
competition on the frontier was normal and often supplied the
highest honors and respect to the victors. It was more than a
display of arms or a simple sport. These backcountry shooting
matches were an external barometer of the frontier's internal
pulse, sorting the weak from the strong.

---

[278] Bernard Bailyn, *The Peopling of British North America: An Introduction*
(New York: Vintage Books, 1986), 111.
[279] Brown, Meredith. *Frontiersman: Daniel Boone and the Making of
America.* Baton Rouge: Louisiana States Universtiy Press, 2008. 10.
[280] Draper, *The Life of Daniel Boone.* 126.
[281] Morgan, *Boone: A Biography.* 37.

According to legend, Daniel won many a match by holding "out his rifle with one hand only and hitting the target."[282] Although the local Catawbas nation was cordial with the white settlers and supplied Daniel with increased observation and tutelage, one Catawba brave grew envious of Daniel's skill and notoriety. Known as Saucy Jack, the Catawba brave lost to Daniel in such competition and resolved "to have no superior alive!"[283] Before the resentful brave could act, however, his intentions reached the ear of Squire Boone, who retorted, "Well, if it has come to this, I'll kill first!"[284] Picking up his hatchet, the formerly quiet Quaker set out in search of the brave.[285] Learning of Squire's response, however, Saucy Jack wisely vanished. Perhaps he feared Daniel's faultless rifle, or perhaps the lion heart of his father. In either case, this anecdote serves to illustrate the loyalty of the Boone family as well as the height of Daniel's fame and great depth of his ability as a hunter and woodsman, which "excited the envy of the friendly and the terror of the hostile Indian."[286]

It also depicts how Daniel learned from his early experiences with Natives. Daniel later wrote

> I often went hunting with [Indians], and frequently gained their applause for my activity at our shooting matches. I was careful not to exceed many of them in shooting, for no people are more envious than they in this sport. I could observe, in their countenances and gestures, the greatest

---

[282] Morgan, *Boone: A Biography*. 39.

[283] Draper, *The Life of Daniel Boone*. 128.

[284] Boome, William P. "Letter from William P. Boone to Lyman Draper, April 27, 1846" in *Draper Manuscripts* 19C1; Lyman Draper interview with Isaiah Boone, 1846, *Draper Manuscripts* 19C61.

[285] Bakeless, *Daniel Boone*. 20.

[286] Draper, *The Life of Daniel Boone*. 128.

expressions of joy when they exceeded me; and, when the reverse happened, envy.[287]

Unlike his fellow hunters and settlers, Daniel was revered by the Native as their brother, hunting companion, and equal. In turn, Daniel seemingly respected their people and their ways.

The Monongahela's Baptism

The glares of war momentarily halted Daniel's profitable forays into the wilderness. By 1754, the weight of the Seven Years' War pressed heavily upon the border settlements of Carolina, Virginia, and Maryland. In January, Virginian Governor Dinwiddie met Major George Washington's alarms of French encroachment upon the Ohio with a letter to President Rowan of North Carolina, "soliciting men to join" the cause to "repel these French aggressors."[288] The French had constructed a fort at the forks of the Ohio—at the convergence point of the Allegheny and Monongahela rivers—with the purpose of controlling the Ohio Country. In 1755, English General Edward Braddock was sent to North American to drive the French from the strategic point of Fort Duquesne. Braddock possessed over thirty-five years of military experience in European war, which proved only disadvantageous to the seasoned General's American campaign.

While stationed in Philadelphia, General Braddock displayed his confidence with Pennsylvania postmaster Benjamin Franklin, stating that he was sure he would take the

---

[287] Boone, Daniel. *The Adventures of Colonel Daniel Boone.* 13.
[288] Draper, *The Life of Daniel Boone.* 128.

fort within two or three days. Franklin retorted with a warning, claiming that the American backwoods was no place for English regulars and that they were in danger of "ambuscades of Indians, who, by constant practice, are dexterous in laying and executing them."[289] Later, Franklin recorded that Braddock

> smil'd at my Ignorance, and reply'd, 'These Savage may indeed be a formidable Enemy to your raw American militia; but upon the King's regular and disciplined Troops, Sir, it is impossible they should make any impression.'

The naïve General declined both Franklin's advice and the assistance of Native scouts.

The Delaware chief Scaroyady—or Monacatootha— wrote to the Governor of Pennsylvania, "A great many of our warriors left [Braddock] & would not be under his Command," for "he looked upon us as dogs and would never hear anything what was said to him." Scaroyady continued

> We often endeavored to advise him, and to tell him of the dangers he was in with his Soldiers, but he never appeared pleased with us.[290]

---

[289] Franklin, Benjamin. *Autobiography.* Barns & Co. Inc., 1944. *152-153.*

[290] Message of Scaroyady conveyed by Conrad Weiser to the governor of Pennsylvania, *Memorandum of Conrad Weiser,"* August 23, 1755, Penn MS, Large Folio, II, Historical Society of Philadelphia, qtd. in *Conrad Wiser*, 390.

From its beginning, the doomed campaign and its reputable English General underestimated the general "rawness" of America's howling wilderness.

Daniel Boone accompanied Braddock's fatal campaign as a teamster, blacksmith, and wagoner at the age of twenty.[291] He joined with one hundred North Carolina troops under Captain Hugh Waddell, who was known for his "energy and bravery." Daniel's task as wagoner was to cut the road and transport the baggage of Braddock's army. This, however, was no simple task. Lyman Draper noted that such a job required the most "unwearied care and patience" to properly conduct the "heavily laden baggage-wagons over the hills and mountains, through streams, ravines, and quagmires" from Fort Cumberland to Fort Duquesne.[292]

The arduous expedition crawled slowly though the American wilderness. George Washington, who served as a Captain on the campaign, wrote to his brother that Braddock's army was "halting to level every Mole Hill, & to erect Bridges over every brook."[293] Additionally, "psychological warfare" continuously plagued the long train of pompous Regulars, as the Natives "pinned the scalps" of the line's outliers "to trees and left the mutilated bodies where they would be seen by Braddock's troops."[294] Unmoved, Braddock stayed his English gaze at Fort Duquesne.

---

[291] Boone, *My Father, Daniel Boone*. 13.

[292] Draper, *The Life of Daniel Boone*, 129.

[293] Ellis, Joseph J. *His Excellency, George Washington.* New York: Vintage Books, 2004. 21.

[294] Ward, Matthew. *Breaking The Backcountry: The Seven Years' War In Virginia And Pennsylvania 1754-1765,* University of Pittsburgh Press; 1 edition (October 17, 2004), 7; Brown, Meredith Mason. *Frontiersman: Daniel Boone and the Making of America.* Baton Rouge: Louisiana States Universtiy Press, 2008. 18.

After weeks of interminable labor, the party of around two thousand passed over the Monongahela River around two o'clock in the afternoon on the memorable July ninth. Lieutenant-Colonel Gage's three hundred and fifty Regulars lead the crossing, followed closely by Sr. John St. Clair's "working party" of two hundred and fifty men. Immediately succeeding the initial force was Braddock's artillery and wagons. The English General placed the petulant militias of Virginia, Maryland, and Carolina dishonorably in the rear, as he believed them unable to possess "courage or good will."[295]

With great ceremony and the Grenadier's March beating their steps—with their "brilliant…dazzling uniforms…burnished arms gleaming in the bright summer's sun"—the chosen army of a little over a thousand troops advanced down the bottleneck of Braddock's Road. In files of three or four men, the company disappeared into the wooded periphery that receded into the great Monongahela. Driven by their honor and pomp, the triumphant Regulars dreamed little of the appalling horror lurking behind every tree. The American wilderness concealed the vicious forces of the great Pontiac of the Ottawas and the Shawanoes chief Cornstalk of Chillicothe. This would be the first of many encounters between Daniel Boone and the Chillicothe family of Cornstalk.

The two forces were positioned in "two ravines heading near each other, with the trail between" them, both attempting to thread the needle for victory.[296] At length, the Natives, waiting in anticipation, poured down on their unsuspecting enemy, "marvel[ing] at the magnificent targets [the British's]

---

[295] Draper, *The Life of Daniel Boone.* 129.
[296] Draper, *The Life of Daniel Boone.* 130.

red coats made."[297] Extreme confusion and anarchy ensued from all sides of the cadaverous valley. Instinctively, the American militia ran to the nearest trees—"firing individually, behind the shelter of tree trunks"—while the British Regulars stood in the clearing, waiting frantically for their commander's orders. Lyman Draper described the scene

> The French and Indians were almost of a man invisible, hidden behind trees, logs, bushes, tall wild grass, and in the deep ravines, save a skulking savage would momentarily rush form his covert to bing down some exposed officer or tear a scalp from some fallen foe, while the half-bewildered soldiery fired their platoons aimlessly into the air or tree-tops.

The universal chaos also spilled out into the baggage trains, for Pontiac's rage spared little. Once the Regulars broke, throwing "away their arms and Ammunition, and even their Cloaths, to escape faster," the waggoners fell under heavy fire.[298] Daniel was one of the few waggoners to live through the hellish barrage. Daniel's son, Nathan, remembered, "When the retreat began [my father] cut his team loose from the wagon and escaped with the horses."[299]

The battle lasted a mere three hours but took over seven hundred and fifty English to a meager thirty-three French and Indian. It was an outright and raw massacre—one that taught its

---

[297] Lofaro, *Daniel Boone.* 14.
[298] Robert Orme, "Journal of General Braddock's Expedition," British Library, 102-107; Ward, Matthew. *Breaking The Backcountry: The Seven Years' War In Virginia And Pennsylvania 1754-1765,* University of Pittsburgh Press; 1 edition (October 17, 2004), 7.
[299] Boone, *My Father, Daniel Boone.* 13.

survivors lessons as deep as the grave. French captive James Smith of our earlier story was forced to witness the ambush from afar, greatly pitying the fallen and the unlucky prisoners. In his memoirs, he wrote, "About sun down I beheld a small party coming in [the fort] with about a dozen prisoners, stripped naked, with their hands tied...and their faces...and bodies...blackened." One by one, continued Smith, the captives were tied naked to pine posts and slowly burned to death with red-hot irons and burning pines branches, the melted sap tearing into their flesh "on the banks of the Allegheny River."[300]

George Washington wrote, the militiamen "behaved like Men and died like Soldiers' while the regulars broke & run as sheep before Hounds."[301] Washington himself buried the fallen General Braddock's body in the "middle of the road and ran wagons over the site to hide the grave," so that "Indians would not scalp and main [his] body."[302] Seventeen years after the massacre, the Presbyterian minister David McClure visited the bloodstained valley and recorded in his journal

It was a melancholy spectacle to see the bones of men strewn over the ground, left to this day, without the solemn rite of sepulture...The bones had been gnawed by wolves, the vestiges of their teeth appearing on them, I examined several, & found the mark of the scalping knife on all.[303]

---

[300] Smith, James. *The Account of Mary Rowlandson.*, 6.

[302] Ellis, *His Excellency, George Washington.* 22; Brown, *Frontiersman: Daniel Boone and the Making of America.* 18.
[303] *Diary of David McClure, Doctor of Divinity*, 1748-1820 (New York: Knickerbocker Press, 1899), 48.

A young man, Daniel learned the import of wisdom within the wilderness and experienced first-hand both the beauties and terrors of the Western country. To his grave, he faulted Braddock's extreme negligence and credited the "want of intelligence and reconnoitering parties" as the "sole cause[s] of the defeat."[304] Nathan Boone later remembered

> [My father] used to censure Braddock's conduct, saying he neglected to keep out spies and flank guards. I think that somehow my father was connected with Washington's colonial troops; he often spoke of Washington, whom both he and my mother personally knew.[305]

The campaign taught Daniel the importance of the Native within the wooded stage of the virgin wilderness. He experienced the particular impact of Amerindian relations upon the success or failure of Western effort and was forever careful never to venture loudly into the woods without an alliance, adequate defense, or bargaining advantage.

Of Romance

After Daniel's baptism by combat, he returned to the peaceful Yadkin Valley and tried to forget the brutish horrors that had filled the great canopies of the western woods. Back in his father's cabin, he took to nature and resumed his pleasures

---

[304] General Kane's *Military History of Great Britain;* Lofaro, Michael A. *Daniel Boone: An American Life.* Lexington: University Press of Kentucky, 2003. 15.
[305] Boone, *My Father, Daniel Boone.* 13.

within her woods. Soon, the serene romance of the Yadkin wilderness acted upon him and sedated his soul. On August 14, 1756, he married Rebecca Bryan—who was described as his equal in everything but the hunt. She was "a woman capable of the hard work and childbearing and dangers, and excitement, of the American frontier" who shared an equal love of and ability within the wilderness. Her nephew, Daniel Bryan, later remembered her as a good bit taller than her husband, "buxom," and of a larger build than the "average woman of the time."[306] Daniel, in contrast, was described as "a sort of pony-built man," about five foot eight inches tall, but as strong as a horse, although one of his hunting companions admitted that he could "lift more than any man I ever saw."[307] Many Boone historians suggest that, while Daniel was away on his many hunts, it was Rebecca that trained their children in marksmanship and woodsmanship. Years later, when Daniel's rheumatism reduced his abilities to mark, Rebecca joined him on his hunts and carried his long rifle.[308]

Rebecca was not unlike Daniel's mother, Sarah Morgan, who was spirited and tough, but also homely and romantic. She was a true frontiersman in her own right, capable of adapting to continuously changing scenery but stable enough to practice "Quaker-like simplicity and propriety" in "all her domestic arrangements."[309] Just as the women of Native cultures were the "masters of [their] own bod[ies], and by … natural right … free to do as [they] pleased," Rebecca was

---

[306] Morgan, *Boone: A Biography.* 49.
[307] Lyman Draper interview with Peter Smith, 1863, *Draper Manuscripts* 18S113; Houston, *A Sketch of the Life and Character of Daniel Boone.* 36.
[308] Lyman Draper interview with Edward Byram, October 2, 1863, *Draper Manuscripts* 19S170.
[309] Morgan, *Boone: A Biography.* 49.

strong and commanding, and she often dominated the authority of the Boone's household.[310]

Between 1756 and 1781, Daniel and Rebecca would have eleven children together—only seven would reach adulthood and only two would outlive their father. But in their union, Daniel found a happy home and a full hearth, sheltered by the quiet valleys of the Yadkin.

It was during his early years with Rebecca that his inner philosophy met his external typography. Daniel's new family settled in a rough cabin in a part of the Yadkin that was described as "The Switzerland of North America," with its "hills gradually swelling into mountains, until the remote portions presented in all directions scenes of wild grandeur and simplicity."[311] With the land's ample supply of game and its gift of sublimity, Daniel's love of the woods grew abundantly along with his love of the family hearth.

Perhaps, it was during this time that Daniel's visions of the West as a supreme hunting ground transposed into his dreams of Eden—a garden to be harvested and enjoyed yet also revered and honored. In a way, Daniel's revised view was antithetical to the European notions of economics and Lockean property. Instead, Daniel's views were singed by romance. They were purely native in origin and exemplified his quixotic blend of settler and native culture and philosophy.

As his family grew, so also grew his dreams of taking them West. The major difference between Daniel and his fellow frontiersman, however, was that Daniel dreamed of settling the

---

[310] Walter O'Meara, *Daughters of the Country: The Women of the Fur Traders and Mountain Men* (New York, 1968), 70.

[311] Reverend F. L. Hanks' lecture before the New York Historical Society, December 1852.

West and not manufacturing a West that was settled. Lyman Draper noted that the borderland of the eighteenth century was a land that contained "a hardy…people," who were "masters of their own free wills."[312] Although Daniel often exhibited a free soul, he appeared to believe that his "free will" and property was forever tethered by the illimitable freedom of nature and its pure society. That, no matter the productive action—labor—or work of mankind, he could neither completely own nor settle the wilderness. Like the stars of the heaven or the meandering breeze of Kentucky's vast valleys, Daniel seemingly believed that the *true* wilderness was forever beyond man's ultimate control.

Such views were averse to the popular natural philosophy of John Locke and his contemporaries. In chapter five of his 1690 *Second Treatise on Government,* Locke declared

> …labour makes the far greatest part of the value of things we enjoy in this world; and the ground which produces the materials is scarce to be reckoned in as any, or at most, but a very small part of it; so little, that even amongst us, land that is left wholly to nature, that hath no improvement of pasturage, tillage, or planting, is called, as indeed it is, waste; and we shall find the benefit of it amount to little more than nothing.[313]

Locke believed the untilled acres of the American wilderness were "waste" because it is only through productive labor that value and enjoyment are instilled within mankind's affairs.

---

[312] Draper, *The Life of Daniel Boone.* 193.
[313] Locke, John. *Second Treatise on Government.* Chapter 5.

Adam Smith concurred with Locke on the importance of labor, writing, "It was not by gold or by silver, but by labor, that all the wealth of the world was originally purchased."[314] The late-eighteenth-century Swiss historian and economist Jean Charles Léonard de Sismondi simplified both Locke's and Smith's assertions on labor and property. In his 1815 work, *Political Economy*, Sismondi wrote, "All that man values is created by his industry."[315]

Like his Native brothers, however, Daniel valued the primordial wilderness. Although he profited from her bounties, Daniel enjoyed the wooded canopy's breathless wind and quiet songs, and he valued her still movements and infinite whispers for their own sake. No application of labor separated his enjoyment from her delights. While the sumptuous bounties of game profited his pockets, by no labor of his own, her intimate pleasures embraced Daniel's soul.

Whether in Penn's woods or deep within the Western Wilderness, Daniel found value in the untouched purity of the woods. Such is the distinction between the enlightened natural philosophy of Western civilization and the rugged and romantic philosophy of nature. While the former concentrates man as the sole instigator and creator of value, enjoyment, and wealth, the latter understands the humble placement of mankind within The Creator's inextricably complex yet beautiful web of interrelationships.

If Daniel's youth among the Pennsylvania Indians impressed upon his soul a love of the untouched woods, then it

---

[314] Smith, Adam. *An Inquiry into the Nature and Causes of the Wealth of Nations.* Edwin Cannan, ed. Chicago: University of Chicago Press, 1976. Book 1, Chapter 5.
[315] J.C.L. Simonde de Sismondi, "Political Economy," 1815, Chapter 2

was during his time of reflection and romance on the Yadkin's banks that taught him that the woods were mystic in nature and called for community, not the solitariness of the long hunter. Maybe it was Braddock's campaign itself that planted this natural seed, a campaign that pinned the height of European civilization against the stature of the natural world and found the former as wanting. Regardless, Daniel's philosophy had been irrevocably changed by his intimate contact with nature and the Native.

CHAPTER 7

Sheltowee, the Revenant

March 1778. Virginia Governor Patrick Henry could not believe his eyes. Scattered upon his desk were militia formation papers, urgent letters from George Washington's encampment at Valley Forge, and correspondence concerning their new French allies, but Governor Henry's attention was fixed on something else. Atop the papers strewn across his Williamsburg desk read the note, "Daniel Boone Captured By Shawnees." The frontier report continued its devastating literature, declaring "all of Boone's party [as] lost."[316]

As governor, Henry was well acquainted with the "distressing" and "deplorable conditions" of Kentucky and understood that, according to his 1777 letter to General Edward Hand, "offensive operations" along with "working on [the Savages] fears" could alone "produce Defense ag. Indians."[317] A strong yet simple colonial presence in Kentucky could provide Henry's western periphery immense security and

---

[316] Faragher, *Daniel Boone.* 167.
[317] "Governor Patrick Henry to General Edward Hand, July 27th, 1777," in *Frontier Defense On The Upper Ohio, 1777-1778,* Reuben Gold Thwaits, Louise Phelps Kellogg, eds., Madison: Wisconsin Historical Society, 1912. 30-31.

advantage. Although it contained a meager fifty settlers in late 1777, Daniel's station on the banks of the Kentucky River—later called Boonesborough—formed a bulwark between the untamed frontier and Henry's Virginia—between the Shawnee and the British.[318]

Henry and his fellow American revolutionaries knew they could not fight a two-front war. In his letter to Colonel William Fleming on February 19, 1778, Governor Henry concluded his plan for the defense of Virginia, blaming the British for inciting the Shawnee against America's western frontiersmen

> I must tell you Sir that I really blush for the occasion of this War with the Shawnee. I doubt not but you detest the vile assassins who have brought it on us at this critical Time when our whole Force was wanted in another Quarter. ...Is not this the work of Tories? No man but an Enemy to American Independence will do it, and thus oblige our People to be hunting after Indians in the Woods, instead of facing Gen. Howe in the field. ...But [the Shawnee] are...Agents for the Enemy, who have taken this method to find employment for the brave back Woodsmen at home, and prevent their joining Gen Washington to strike a decisive stroke for Independency at this critical time.[319]

---

[318] Draper, Lyman. *Lyman Draper's Manuscripts*, 4B118-ED, 125-Ed.
[319] "Governor Patrick Henry to Colonel William Fleming, February 19th, 1778," in *Frontier Defense On The Upper Ohio, 1777-1778,* Reuben Gold Thwaits, Louise Phelps Kellogg, eds., Madison: Wisconsin Historical Society, 1912. 205-209.

Henry, no doubt, blamed the British for Daniel's capture, as Daniel's success establishing a permanent American fort in the frontier indirectly posed a great threat to British control.

By April, numerous reports returned from Boonesborough, exposing its population as "a poor, distressed, half-naked, half-starved people."[320] Their great leader, pathfinder, and friend had been killed or captured by the Shawnee—the latter being the worse of the two—and the fort subsequently fell into disarray. Fearing the worst, Daniel's family headed back east, as Daniel's Virginian rivals vied for command of the fort. The newly formed vacuum of power fomented unrest and instability.

Western historian Stephen Aaron writes, "Deprived of alternative fare and tormented by Indians, pioneers lived 'on their guns' and turned to men like Boone to feed them and lead them." Daniel Boone was "a hero in hunting and warfare;" he founded, led, and defended Kentucky's first settlement; but now he was supposed as dead and so also seemed Boonesborough and the western cause.[321]

Of Sorrow

After his exploration of Kentucky with John Findley in 1769, Daniel resolved to move his family west. Although he returned from his near-two-year journey empty-handed, he did not return without profit. The woods of *Kanta-ke* greatly nourished him. Perhaps Daniel learned what modern American poet Sophia Cabot Black put in words, "Nature loves and makes

---

[320] Faragher, *Daniel Boone.* 166.
[321] Aaron, *How the West Was Lost.* 29-30.

you love." Perhaps, this love is also what brought him back to the Yadkin. For over two years he had explored *Kanta-ke* and its many wonders but, for the next two years, Daniel's history is silent.

Within the many histories of Boone, little is written about his return from Kentucky in May, 1771 and the Boone family's initial push into Kentucky in early 1773. One imagines Daniel dreaming of the verdurous *Kanta-ke* during this period, but his feet remained planted in the Yadkin. The wonders of the West certainly occupied his thoughtful and restive mind, but his wanderlust was momentarily wander-less.

Some historians suggest that he remained busy on the family farm. Others, however, postulate that he escaped the Yadkin during frequent but short hunts in search of "suitable country for a new settlement."[322] John Bakeless argued that Daniel spent most of 1772 traveling from one Cherokee village to the next, dwelling with them in "wigwams, hunting with braves" and "talking with the chiefs."[323]

Lyman Draper theorized that during one of these winter adventures in early 1773, Daniel, along with Benjamin Cutbirth and "a few others," explored central Kentucky and were "greatly pleased with the country."[324] Daniel had dreamed of *Kanta-ke* from his youth amidst Penn's woods, and his impatience was growing. He heard of other pioneering ventures into Kentucky, one led by the McAfee brothers in early June 1773, who were "fired by the glowing description of the beauty and fertility of Kentucky," and others led by James Harrod.[325]

---

[322] Draper, *The Life of Daniel Boone.* 283.
[323] Bakeless, *Daniel Boone.* 67.
[324] Draper, *The Life of Daniel Boone.* 284; Bakeless, *Daniel Boone.* 67.
[325] O'Brien, Michael, I. *Irish Pioneers in Kentucky.* CreateSpace Independent Publishing Platform, 2014.

Kentucky's popularity was rapidly growing, and Benjamin Franklin himself lobbied London for the "right to buy much of the lands ceded by the Iroquois" to construct a new province called Vandalia.[326] Stirred by the passing opportunity to explore an open frontier, Daniel returned to his Yadkin farm for the last time in early spring and resolved to pack up his family and make haste to the West.

History is unclear why Rebecca Boone had hitherto been against moving west until now. Perhaps her mind was changed when their oldest son, James, turned sixteen and proved able to provide a hand in the arduous journey. Perhaps Daniel's impassioned accounts of *Kanta-ke* finally affected Rebecca's deeply romantic soul. John Mason Peck, a contemporary of Boone, commented

> the wives of our western pioneers are as courageous, and as ready to enter on the line of march to plant the germ of a new settlement as their husbands.[327]

Rebecca's fiery and strong character may prove truth to the latter, for "the patient, fearless Rebecca was ready now…to follow her man where [he] chose to go."[328]

Daniel sold his farm on the Yadkin in 1773 and prepared to lead his family west into the wilderness of Kentucky. While Bostonians dumped tea into the harbor and Thomas Jefferson drafted the precursor to the Declaration of

---

[326] Rice, Otis. *Frontier Kentucky*, University Press of Kentucky: Second Edition (July 20, 1993) 7-54.
[327] Peck, *Life of Daniel Boone*. 21.
[328] Bakeless, *Daniel Boone*. 69.

Independence, Daniel, alone on the edge of civilization, sharpened his axe to enter into a world unknown.

One may imagine the sheer ecstasy he received from the affair, since from his youth he sought any excuse possible to neglect his tedious farming duties for the freedom of the woods. On September 25, 1773, Daniel, along with his brother's family and a party of their close friends, "bade farewell" to the Yadkin's farmed fields and turned toward *Kanta-ke.*[329] Lyman Draper highlights this moment in Daniel's history as one that displayed the height of the Boone family's wanderlust. He writes

> Fifty-six years before, Squire Boone, with his parents, had bid adieu to friends and kindred in England and set sail for the New World; thirty-three years later, Squire Boone with his family, including his son Daniel, set out from Pennsylvania for the Yadkin country; and now, after a lapse of twenty-three years, we find Daniel Boone, true to the instincts of his family, as the head of a little band of poor but fearless, enterprising men seeking quiet homes in a distant wilderness.[330]

Daniel's widowed mother accompanied the westward party for half of the day before returning to her home on the Yadkin. Both mother and son knew that such a goodbye was probably their last and one could only imagine the emotion such a moment carried. Daniel was his mother's son, reared equally by her Quaker patience and fortitude as her ancient Welsh romance and emotion. From her example, he learned to revere

---

[329] Houston, *A Sketch of the Life and Character.* 12.
[330] Draper, *The Life of Daniel Boone.* 285.

life, find joy in the little things, and hear the silent song of the wilderness. In his 1842 letter to his grandson, Daniel's friend and hunting companion Peter Houston remembered the supreme emotion of this moment

> And when a halt was called for a separation they threw their arms around each other's neck and tears flowed freely from all eyes. Even Daniel, in spite of his brave and manly heart was seen to lift the lapel of his pouch to dry the tears from his eyes whilst his dear old mother held around his neck weeping bitterly.[331]

Daniel is only recorded to have wept openly on few occasions, and their parting spared no tears.

Unlike the comparatively luxurious pioneers of the nineteenth century, who conveyed their family and belongings in covered wagons and on trodden and tested roads, Daniel's party followed a mere trace that skirted through rugged and untamed wilderness. They carried everything that their journey and settlement required on their belts and backs. The frontiersmen of this era were known to carry haversacks, filled with both jerked meat and johnnycakes. Historian Ted Franklin Belue describes the jerking process in his work, *The Long Hunt*

> To jerk meat, hunters cut four forked saplings three to six feet tall and stuck them into the ground. Then they placed poles lengthwise in the forks and sticks across the poles three to four inches apart. They sliced the meat with the grain into strips half an inch thick, weighing up to a pound

---

[331] Houston, *A Sketch of the Life and Character*. 12.

each, laid the strips on the rack, and kindled a fire underneath. ...Smoking might take two days.[332]

Boone historian Michael Lofaro writes, "Extraordinary difficulties marked their migration," for the "route was a serpentine hunter's trace that was too narrow for a wagon."[333] Some walked, some rode the packhorses, but all struggled over the three tumultuous mountain ranges of the early west: the Powells, Waldens, and Cumberlands.

Stephen Aaron describes the Trans-Appalachian journey as a true "test of toughness," as "the trip itself, over the steepest mountains and through some of the densest, wettest forests in eastern North America, was arduous," to say the least.[334] The eager party trekked over the nearby Horton's Summit and Powells Mountain, passing the Clinch River and its high mountain range. Although laden with goods and slowed by women and children, the party made good time—a hundred miles in the first two weeks. Thomas Carter of the Clinch River later remembered the party's passing, recalling the great and "terrible racket" their woman and children caused.[335]

Near the western base of Walden's Ridge, "where Powell's River flows along a lovely vale," the forward party pitched camp and "awaited the arrival of the rear."[336] Earlier in their journey, Daniel had dispatched his oldest son, James Boone, and a small party of his comrades on a dual mission of both notifying Captain Russell of Castle Woods of their party's

[332] Belue, Ted Franklin, *The Long Hunt.* 89.
[333] Lofaro, *Daniel Boone.* 41.
[334] Aaron, *How the West Was Lost.* 24.
[335] Woods, M.B. Letter to Lyman Draper, April 9, 1883, *Draper Manuscripts* 4C26.
[336] Draper, *The Life of Daniel Boone.* 285.

western migration and procuring a load of flour for their journey. The small party successfully completed their mission and their fully packed mules were additionally complemented by a small drove of cattle—a gift of twenty-six in total from Captain Russell.[337] The mission was only supposed to consume a day and distance the two groups by no more than a couple miles.

Young Boone speedily drove the party to meet the main group by the following evening. The night of October 9 overtook them, however, and the small band camped on the "northern bank of Walden's Creek," modern day U.S. Highway 68. They were unaware that the main party was a mere three miles ahead of them, and they were "equally unaware that their steps were silently shadowed by a force of Indians."[338] As the sun rose around them and, as they were "locked in the sweet embrace of balmy sleep," the unconscious group was ambushed by a group of Delaware and Shawnee Indians. The Mendinall boys were killed immediately—they were the lucky ones. Both James Boone and Henry Russell were shot in the hip, forced to defend themselves from the barrage of tomahawks and knives with only their hands, seizing the naked blades to save their lives.

Already dismembered and bleeding profusely, James Boone was tortured by the attackers. They slowly ripped out his finger and toe nails and cut his body piece by piece. The Natives had little time for their proper "burning at the stake, but they did pretty well with their knives" until death, "like an angel of mercy," came to their captive's relief.[339] In his last agonizing

---

[337] Houston, *A Sketch of the Life and Character*. 12.
[338] Draper, *The Life of Daniel Boone*. 287; Lofaro, *Daniel Boone*. 42.
[339] Bakeless, *Daniel Boone*. 71; Draper, *The Life of Daniel Boone*. 287.

moments, James' cries searched for his mother but his shrieks were of no avail. At last his skull was beaten in with the blunt edge of the tomahawk, his body "slashed to ribbons" and pierced with a multitude of arrows.[340]

His body strewn across the forest floor, James' death was to serve as more than a deterrent from western settlement, it was also to serve as a poignant warning to all western settlers of the pain and vile horror that lurked behind every tree. What was left of their bodies was discovered later that morning by a member of Daniel's party. The boys' remains were collected in linen sheets and buried under a log—so as not to be disturbed by wolves. Twenty years later, one of the boy's bones was found "wedged between two rock ledges" with his "skull split" in two.[341]

Dejected and deeply depressed, Daniel sullenly led the party back to the Clinch River and to the safety of their Yadkin Valley. For the moment, Daniel's dream "slipped from his grasp," and his hopes of bringing his family West were splintered beneath the weight of the wilderness.[342]

Henry's slave was hidden in the nearby bushes during the ambush and witnessed the entirety of this heart-rending scene. He was so impacted by the gruesome episode that he wandered aimlessly in the woods for eleven days before he came to. Later he recounted that, during James' screams, James pleaded with the Natives that his father was their friend and ally and begged for relief. The sad truth is that the Native that led

---

[340] Bakeless, *Daniel Boone.* 72.
[341] Hagy, James William. "The First Attempt to Settle Kentucky: Boone in Virginia," Filson Club Historical Quarterly 53 (July 1979): 227-33.
[342] Lofaro, *Daniel Boone.* 43.

the barrage was actually a Shawnee brave named Big Jim, whom James was intimately acquainted with.

Nathan Boone, Daniel's youngest son, later remembered that Big Jim often frequented the Boone homestead in North Carolina and spent many nights under their roof as a friend and companion. It is unclear whether Big Jim ever recognized James during the immense havoc or whether the cadaverous and bloodstained campsite spurred him forever on regardless of his past dealings with the Boones. In either case, the bloody episode highlights the strength and direction of the Native mind: they would go to the extreme to protect their hunting ground, and if you challenged their way of life, they would challenge yours. Daniel Boone never forgot this painful lesson.

A Road in the Wilderness

Repose and farm labor seemed to plague Daniel's life. The winter of 1773-74 is unrecorded in Boone history, although it appears from county records that he wintered his family in David Gass's cabin on the Clinch River. The failed venture westward beat him physically, emotionally, and financially. Whatever profit he made from selling his farm before the journey was now depleted and his family was without a home. Preserved by contemporary descriptions, one traveler remembered Daniel during this time. He wrote, "Boone was dressed in deer-skin colored black, and had his hair plaited and clubbed up."[343] This description painted Daniel in a rough blend of Anglo-Native cultures, with the deerskin colored black like

---

[343] Bakeless, *Daniel Boone.* 74-75.

the Native mixed with the plaited hairstyle popular in Europe. For the moment, Daniel's appearance mirrored his position: torn between his civilization and the West.

Although most of the party returned to their homes or families on the Yadkin, Daniel appeared to never have ventured east of the Clinch. Perhaps he was afraid that, like the Israelites passing over the river Jordan or Lot's wife turning her gaze once more upon Sodom, if he returned east to the Yadkin, he would never return to his *Kanta-ke*. In the spring, Daniel alone ventured back to the Powell Valley to visit the grave of his son. Pushing aside the logs, he uncovered James' blond hair, the crusted blood still evident on his mutilated features. The trembling father removed the pieces of his son from the rough grave and dug it deeper, placing the log covering back in its original place, a makeshift gravestone. About that time, a great storm rumbled the heavens and

> during its continuance, from the melancholy associations and gloominess of the place, mingled with the dismal howlings of the storm, Boone felt more dejected, as he used afterwards to relate, than he ever did in all his life.[344]

Perhaps Daniel felt alone for the first time in his life, his external environment echoing his internal pain. In the past, the wilderness provided solitude, solace, and an outlet for his soul. That night, as the rain poured heavily upon his fireless camp and the thunder boomed throughout the wooded canopy, Daniel remembered only his pain and suffering.

---

[344] Draper, *The Life of Daniel Boone.* 304.

The following year brought hope. In March 1775, Daniel himself drew the boundaries of Kentucky in the Watauga Treaty—also known as the Sycamore Shoals Treaty—signed between the Transylvania Land Company and the Cherokee Indians.[345] The Cherokee alone held "colorable claims" in Kentucky, as the Iroquois had relinquished their claims of the Ohio Valley in their 1768 Treaty of Fort Stanwix and the Shawnee forfeited their claims in the Battle of Point Pleasant in 1774.[346]

The American pioneer and merchant Richard Henderson dreamed up the treaty's particulars. In his early-twentieth-century account, *Boonesborough: Its Founding, Pioneer Struggles, Indians Experiences, Transylvania Days, and Revolutionary Annals,* George W. Ranck described Henderson as "rather showy," although a man of "genuine ability and culture." Henderson led the negotiations in present day Elizabethton, Tennessee, which was "familiar to the Indians, in a valley that has long been known for its fertility and beauty."[347] The contract supplied money and goods—£10,000 in total—to the Cherokee Indians in return for most of present day Kentucky and Tennessee—a total of twenty million acres.

Atticulaculla, considered as "the Solon of his day," headed the Cherokee's negotiations. Nicknamed *Little Carpenter,* Atticulaculla, like "a white carpenter," could "make every notch and joint fit in wood, so he could bring all his views

---

[345] Houston, *A Sketch of the Life and Character.* 13.
[346] Brown, *Frontiersman.* 68.
[347] Ranck, George Washington. *Boonesborough: Its Founding, Pioneer Struggles, Indian Experiences, Transylvania Days, and Revolutionary Annals.* Louisville: John P. Morton & Company, 1901. 4; 7.

to fill and fit their places in the political machinery of his nation."[348] Henderson's plan was to establish a fourteenth colony—a land for the hardworking and brave poor—charging perpetual rent and preserving his rights within the government. An audacious land grab, Henderson's plan required extreme secrecy. As North Carolinian Governor Josiah Martin later wrote, it was "daring, unjust, and unwarranted," let alone "illicit and fraudulent," as Kentucky already belonged to the Earl of Granville.[349]

If made public, the plan would fall under the scrutiny of colonial officials and become open to rivals. Such secrecy was not uncommon in the early American West, however. George Washington himself wrote to his land agent in the Ohio Valley to conduct their "operation...under the guise of hunting game."[350] Albeit, in his January 1775 letter to Andrew Miller, the deputy auditor of North Carolina Archibald Neilson inquired, "Pray is Dick Henderson out of his head?"[351]

It is unclear whether Daniel supported the treaty, although one could imagine that his colorful descriptions of Kentucky molded Henderson's visions into reality. Regardless, the woodman's presence at the negotiations, although limited, was advantageous due to his intimate relations with the Overhill Indians. They seemed to trust him and he trusted them. Although indirect, the treaty's illicit peace with the Cherokee and the fraudulent financial backing of Henderson's company provided a great lift to Daniel's failed dreams. With Henderson,

---

[348] Walker, *Felix Walker's Narrative*. 2.
[349] Bakeless, *Daniel Boone.*. 84.
[350] Washington, George, "The Creative Forces in Westward Expansion: Henderson and Boone," *American Historical Review, 20* (October 1914): 100.
[351] Henderson, Archibald. *The Star of Empire: Phases of the Western Movement in the Old Southwest*. Durham: The Seeman Printery, 1919. 54.

Daniel obtained the means necessary to finally migrate his family into *Kanta-ke.*

Before the treaty discussions even commenced, Daniel had already procured a body of fellow woodsmen near Long Island on the Holston River to settle *Kanta-ke.* Leaving his brother Squire in charge of their ready band, Daniel ran off to Watauga to attend the treaty's preliminary negotiations. It seems that Daniel was going to embark into *Kanta-ke* with or without Henderson.

Although many Cherokee leaders favored the treaty, a true consensus was never reached. Most of the tribes present at the negotiation hunted the lands they ceded but their towns were "at some distance from Henderson's proposed colony and ideally would remain so."[352] The famous Cherokee diplomat Oconostata prophesied

> This is but the beginning…the invader has crossed the great sea in ships; he has not been stayed by broad rivers, and now he has penetrated the wilderness and overcome the ruggedness of the mountains. Neither will he stop here. He will force the Indian steadily before him across the Mississippi ever towards the west…till the red man be no longer a roamer of the forests and a pursuer of wild game.[353]

It was the Chickamagua Cherokee and son of Atticulaculla, *Tyi.yu Gansi.ni,* or Dragging Canoe, that providing the foreboding foresight that history has most remembered. Taking Daniel by the hand, he declared, "Brother, we have given you a

---

[352] Aaron, *How the West Was Lost.* 35.
[353] Bakeless, *Daniel Boone.* 87.

fine land, but I believe you will have much trouble settling it." Dragging Canoe appears to have understood the Lockean mistake better than anyone at Watauga. Owning and settling are two completely different things, not won by deed or title, but natural right and reciprocity.

Before storming out of the conference in protest, Dragging Canoe peered deep into his brother's eyes and took Daniel aside, warning that "there [is] a dark cloud over that country."[354] No white man at Watauga knew the infinite and immediate depth of Dragging Canoe's premonition. Undaunted by his brother's warnings and driven forever by his deep wanderlust, Daniel steadied his gaze upon *Kanta-ke* and rendezvoused with his band on the Holston. He had witnessed the pride and force of the Native during Braddock's campaign and James' death, but he pushed on regardless.

Historian George W. Ranck concluded that Daniel kept his family near the Warrior's Path because he never gave up his vision of settling Kentucky. On March 17, 1775, without a harmonious Cherokee blessing or even Daniel in attendance, Henderson concluded the treaty negotiations, his anxious woodsman already seven days into *Kanta-ke*.

By the tenth of March 1775, the ring of axes filled the western forest. The building of the Wilderness Road had begun. Its purpose was to cut a rough road to the Kentucky River through the trackless wilderness to alleviate the supreme burdens of familial transportation and settlement into the West. It would run from the Holston Valley in Tennessee to future Boonesborough in central Kentucky. Fellow axeman and hunter

---

[354] Bakeless, *Daniel Boone.* 87; Haywood, John. *The Civil and Political History of the State of Tennessee* (Knoxville: Heiskell and Brosn, 1803), 58-59.

Felix Walker later remembered, "By general consent," we "put ourselves under the management and control of Col. Boon, who was to be our pilot and conductor through the wilderness."[355]

Daniel's band of thirty hardened men blazed through Powell's Valley—passing James Boone's log grave—and on through the Cumberland Gap with relative ease. Once they reached Daniel's old Warrior's Path, they set out to enlarge the ancient trace for a near fifty-mile stint, "threading" the "sublime defile" that later became known as Boone's Gap.[356] They then passed through Hazel Patch, turning west toward the Rockcastle River. Felix Walker remembered

> On leaving [Rockcastle River], we had to encounter and cut our way through a country of about twenty miles, entirely covered with dead brush, which we found a difficult and laborious task.[357]

A mere three weeks after they left the Holston, the party erupted from the dense cane and beheld the "pleasing and rapturous appearance of the plains of Kentucky," remembered Walker. Entirely captivated, Walker wrote in his narrative

> So rich a soil we had never seen before; covered with clover in full bloom, the woods were abounding with wild game—turkeys so numerous that it might be said they appeared but one flock, universally scattered in the woods. It appeared that nature, in the profusion of her bounty, had spread a feast for all that lives, both for the animal and

---

[355] Walker, *Felix Walker's Narative*. 3.
[356] Ranck, *Boonesborough*. 10.
[357] Walker, *Felix Walker's Narrative*. 3.

rational world. A sight so delightful to our view and grateful to our feelings, almost inclined us, in imitation of Columbus, in transport to kiss the soil of Kentucky, as he hailed and saluted the sand on his first setting his foot on the shores of America.

Although *Kanta-ke's* beauty and sumptuous bounty blessed Daniel before, one could only imagine the sheer delight and ecstasy this moment produced in his soul. Never before had *Kanta-ke's* supreme sublimity enveloped him with such hope, peace, and community. For the first time in his life, Daniel's purpose changed and his compass altered. He was not on one of his long hunts and his trap line did not govern his path. Rather, his purpose was to bring his family West and his compass duly pointed toward the setting sun. However, "man may appoint, but One greater than men can disappoint," remembered Felix Walker.[358]

March 24, 1775. Daniel's party was within fifteen miles of their destination, near the "mouth of one of [the Kentucky River's] tributary streams, which was known then as Otter Creek."[359] Amidst the undulating countryside of modern-day Richmond, Kentucky, the company camped for the night on the banks of the Hays and Hart Forks of Silver Creek. As their fire receded with the darkness, "a volley from the woods" interrupted their slumber.[360] The confusion exploded in the dawn's silence, with tomahawks and lead piercing Kentucky's crisp early morning air.

---

[358] Walker, *Felix Walker's Narrative*. 5.
[359] Ranck, *Boonesborough*. 9.
[360] Bakeless, *Daniel Boone*. 91.

The barrage created a havoc so complete that Daniel's brother Squire seized his coat in place of his powder horn and Daniel himself scrambled half-naked around the campsite. One man fell headlong into the fire's hot coals, like game on a spit. The smell of burnt flesh and hair was quickly overwhelmed by the distinct smell of battle—blood mixed evenly with the dark fumes of powder and fear. A bullet twisted through the cartilage of Captain Twitty's knees and Felix Walker was badly wounded. The attack lasted for only a moment. By the time Daniel and his men steadied their spirits, the battle was over and the woods quiet.

As spirited and vigorous as the phantoms struck, so they receded into the darkness. Panting and panicked, the party stood still on the bloody ground and waited for a resurgent attack. But the wood's silence was dull and eerie as they surveyed the dead that covered their small campsite. Silence fell upon them as though an icy winter blanket, but no further attack came.

The shock-warfare frayed the party's nerves and tore many of their bodies to pieces. Although seemingly unfinished, the attack had fulfilled its mission. Later that morning, a small group of pathfinders made their way back down the trail they created the weeks prior and headed back to the relative safety of Anglo settlement.

Although unscathed from the battle, Daniel was not untouched. Two years prior, his entrance into *Kanta-ke* was thwarted by a Delaware and Shawnee war party; today, it was the Cherokee. Daniel lost his son in the first and his men in the latter, but the similarities of these battles only later became fully known to him. Just as his friend and ally Big Jim had conducted the previous massacre, it is believed that Dragging Canoe himself led this assault of the latter.[361] It appears that Dragging Canoe's "dark cloud" premonition of *Kanta-ke* was less of a vision than a forewarning.[362]

Felix Walker remembered, "Hope vanished from most of us, and left us suspended in the tumult of uncertainty and conjecture."[363] After a number of days, Twitty passed, although Daniel worked hard to heal his wounds with the wooded medicinals he learned from his youth among Penn's Natives.

Pushing forward, the reduced party transported Felix Walker the remaining fifteen miles on a litter to the banks of the Kentucky River—thirty miles distant of modern-day Lexington. On April 5, 1775, the work was at last finished—the prophecy of the Wilderness Road was realized—and the tired and tattered party arrived at their destination. The very next day, Daniel's party was "hard at work at Boonesborough."[364]

Richard Henderson understood that everything now "depended in Boone's maintaining his ground—at least until [reinforcements] could get there." Felix Walker credited Daniel's "firmness" and "fortitude" for their station's success, writing that "Colonel Boone conducted the company under his care through the wilderness, with great propriety, intrepidity and courage."[365] Daniel's determination and fortitude was crucial to the settlement's early success.

On April 18, however, Henderson arrived at Boone's station and was immediately disgusted at the progress of the

---

[361] Arnow, Harriette Simpson, *Seedtime on the Cumberland.* New York, 1960, 172-202.
[362] Haywood, John. *The Civil and Political History of the State of Tennessee* (Knoxville: Heiskell and Brosn, 1803), 58-59.
[363] Walker, *Felix Walker's Narrative.* 6.
[364] Bakeless, *Daniel Boone.* 93.
[365] Walker, *Felix Walker's Narrative.* 7.

fort. Although Daniel led a successful venture into the wilderness, he and his men were so enamored with Kentucky and its many bounties that they had spent little time surveying or building the fort's defenses. Instead, they went hunting.

Henderson quickly took charge and moved the fort's location "a little farther up the river bank."[366] Although he displayed an external commanding front, he privately rebuke his "damned recruits," who he described as a "set of scoundrels who scarcely believe in God of fear the devil."[367] Henderson's chosen location was "much higher" than Daniel's original campsite and perched on the Kentucky River's plateau, overlooking the many Sycamores of the fertile bottomland. Early-nineteenth-century Western historian John Mason Peck remembered the construction of the fort, writing

> [it] was built in the form of a parallelogram, and was about two hundred and fifty feet broad. Houses of hewn logs, built in a square form, projected form each corner, adjoining which were stockades for a short distance; and the remaining space on the four sides, except the gateways, was filled up with cabins, erected of rough logs, placed close together, which made a sure defense. The gates, or doorways, were on opposite sides, constructed of slabs of timber, split several inches in thickness, and hung with stout wooden hinges.[368]

[366] Bakeless, *Daniel Boone.* 99.
[367] Henderson, Richard. "Judge Richard Henderson's Journal of a Trip to 'Cantuckey' and of Events at Boonesborough in 1775," in Ranck, George Washington, *Boonesborough: Its Founding, Pioneer Struggles, Indian Experiences, Transylvania Days, and Revolutionary Annals.* Louisville: John P. Morton & Company, 1901. 173.
[368] Peck, *Life of Daniel Boone.* 27-28.

Daniel's inability—or lack of desire—to lead the fort's construction speaks to his nature as a woodsman and quasi-Indian. He held little interest in the production of civilization. The fort's—or *Borough's*—construction was attributed to "Boone's confidence in [the people] and [theirs] in him," although internally, Daniel had little interest in the fort's erection.[369] In his *Narrative,* Felix Walker wrote, the fact that "no person did actually command entirely" impressed one Boonesborough visitor in 1775 as "all anarchy and confusion."[370] From all accounts, although Richard Henderson attempted to lead and build the fort, it was Daniel's character, expertise, and position among his fellow frontiersman that molded the fort's many parts into a stable community, not civilization.

By June 13, 1775, Boonesborough was ready for more settlers, although John C. Abbott maintained it was not until the following day.[371] Daniel was in a hurry to bring his beloved Rebecca and their seven children into Kentucky, although the previous day—June 12, 1775—Henderson wrote in a personal letter that Boonesborough was no place for "growing family."[372] Daniel infused his family with his wanderlust, courage, and love of the untamed West and they, like him, longed for its embrace. Henderson's opinion aside, the Boones were finally moving west.

After a sublime autumnal journey, the united family concluded their five-hundred-mile tour of the true wilderness—

[369] Ranck, *Boonesborough.* 21.
[370] Walker, *Felix Walker's Narrative.* 163.
[371] Abbott, *Daniel Boone.* 127.
[372] Henderson, Richard. "Letter of Judge Henderson (June 12, 1775) to Proprietors Remaining in North Carolina," in *Boonesborough; Its Founding, Pioneer Struggles, Indian Experiences, Transylvania Days, and Revolutionary Annals,* by George Washington Ranck, 189.

hundreds of miles beyond the line of Anglo-American settlement—and arrived at Boonesborough at the beginning of September. For the first time, Rebecca saw the land that Daniel had spent years courting. Although a tough and tried frontiersman's wife, she had yet to behold the true frontier. Her thoughts upon reaching Daniel's *Kanta-ke* and its fertile rivers and plains are beyond estimation. Perhaps by journey's end, *Kanta-ke's* serene beauty and seemingly peaceful sublimity quelled all the envy and pain that Daniel's extended absences had produced in her over the many years. Perhaps not. Either way, the Boones were finally together.

The Chase

The Sabbath on the frontier was like every other day. The only established churches were each family's hearth and, even then, there was always work to do or sleep to be had. Frontier life was difficult. If you planted corn, the Natives burned it, and if you hunted outside of the fort's walls, the Natives hunted you. In April of 1776, one surveyor was killed by the Mingoes, while two others were captured and tortured by the Shawnee of the Ohio. On July 7, another hunter was killed by a watchful party of Shawnees. On many occasions, hunters left the fort and never returned. Such events instilled so great a fear throughout Kentucky that Colonel William Russel advised all settlements in Kentucky to be abandoned. The Natives were winning.

While the American Continental Congress was pressed hard at their work on Sunday July 14th, 1776, Daniel Boone took a nap. General George Washington beckoned for supplies, men, and adequate funding but all Daniel Boone needed was some rest. Earlier that day, Daniel's daughter had pierced the sole of her foot on a swath of cut cane. Jemima was fourteen years old and nicknamed "Duck," for her great love of the water. While her dad rested, Jemima joined Elizabeth (Betsy) and Frances (Fanny) Callaway in a dug-out canoe and paddled down the river, sticking her foot in the cool water to ease the pain.

We can imagine the hushed laughter and joy that filled the girls' canoe as they drifted peacefully downriver. Frontier life was hard, but these girls were making the most of it. Nearly a quarter mile downstream and as the raft drifted close to the northern bank's rocky cliffs, a group of five Natives appeared near the shore. Emerging from *Kanta-ke's* thick cane, they rushed at the girls. Frantic, Fanny struck the first brave with her paddle and Betsy clubbed with her fists. Jemima screamed in hopes that the warning would be heard in Boonesborough. Although brave, the captives' efforts were of no avail and they were rushed to the shore.

Their captors quickly cut the bottom of their dresses so that the girls could move more easily through the dense cane and forest and threatened the girls with scalping, if they proved difficult. Historian Robert Morgan noted that the girls employed the scrapped clothes around their "legs to protect them from briars and limbs." From this account, it would seem the girls were prepared for the worst—a long and arduous journey through the thick woods at break-neck speeds. Daniel Bryan later claimed that the Natives chose "ground where they would make the least trail" and, although the "girls would mash down a weed" on the trail to mark their path, the Natives would quickly "straighten it up or turn it the other way."[373]

---

[373] Morgan, Robert. *Boone, A Biography.* 203

The Native party consisted of three Shawnee and two Cherokee warriors who were on their way home from a Cherokee conference at the town of Chota, arranged by Dragging Canoe and intent on "denouncing the white settlement."[374] Their leader was a Cherokee chief named Hanging Maw, who knew the Boone family well, for he had spent time with the Boones while they were on the Watagua, a couple years prior. Recognizing Jemima, Hanging Maw inquired about the other two girls. Jemima asserted that they were all Boones, believing that, if Hanging Maw considered them all the daughters of his friend, he would spare their lives. Hanging Maw laughed, "Yes, we have done pretty well for old Boone this time."[375]

It is important to note that kidnapping was understood very differently by Natives than by whites. With upwards of ninety-percent of their numbers decimated by disease and war, Native populations thrived on the acculturation of their captives. Not only would Hanging Maw be rewarded by the heroic capture, but these three Boone girls would make three great Shawnees.

Hanging Maw's friendship with Boone did not dissuade the party nor did it slow their pace. They pushed for two days without stopping for food and only halting for nightly rest. Around nine o'clock on the morning of July 16th, many miles from Boonesborough and just passed the Hinkston's Forks just thirteen miles from the Upper Blue Licks, the braves killed a buffalo and enjoyed their first meal.

But Jemima's screams shook Daniel from his Sunday slumber, and little did the braves know that they were being

---

[374] Morgan, Robert. *Boone, A Biography.* 204.
[375] Draper, Lyman. *The Life of Daniel Boone.* 413.

hunted. Daniel had sent parties up and down the river to ascertain the captor's tracks and he even sent another group to the Blue Licks to cut off the Natives' path over the Ohio River. Although his leadership was never questioned, some Boone historians argue that Daniel's orders were intended to separate his forces so that he could stealthily track the girls himself.

Daniel and a small group of his most-trusted companions, John Findley included, sifted through the thick cane of *Kanta-ke,* making five miles on the first day. On the second, Daniel seemed to lose their tracks and was forced to make a tough decision—bleed precious time backtracking some distance to re-identify the tracks or direct his team's force forward toward where he knew the Natives would be. There are many stories of Daniel Boone that demonstrate both his woodsmanship and understanding of indigenous wisdom. With the lives of Jemima and the Callaway girls on the line, however, this decision was monumental. Daniel believed he knew *Kanta-ke* as well as a people who hunted within her bounds for thousands of years. He knew where they were going without knowing where they were. The truly incredible thing was that he was right.

Daniel's party pushed forward, leaving the girls' tracks behind and, after zig-zagging from one buffalo trace to another, they hurdled the fallen buffalo. Daniel knew the Natives would cross from one trace to another to confuse anyone in pursuit. Standing only thirty yards from the unsuspecting warriors, Daniel's party fanned into position. The braves were busy cooking their buffalo feast and Fanny remembered that, while watching Big Jimmy "spitting up meat," blood "burst out of his breast before she heard the gun."

Daniel's attack began with the aimless report of William Smith's rifle, who later claimed that his premature shot was in self-defense. Regardless, this forced Findley to shoot at the Shawnee's sentinel and created a deadly confusion. One of Daniel's men nearly beat Betsy to death with the butt of his rifle and the obscuring cloud of gunfire allowed a number of braves to escape. Albeit uncoordinated, the rescue attempt was successful and the girls returned to the safety of their families within Boonesborough.

Years later, Daniel learned that the Shawnee brave he killed during the skirmish was the son of Blackfish, the main character of our next story.

'Salt and Sheltowee'

After every sunrise comes the sunset and, true to form, Boonesborough experienced many a dark night. By the end of 1777, the racked and starved fort was devoid of hope and its precious salt. Geographic isolation mixed with continuous Native barrages compounded the settlers' already infinite difficulties, raping their fields of precious corn and staying their hunters' attention on the defense. Hundreds of miles past the defined line of white settlement the exposed station subsisted on its dangerous harvest of wild meat, papaws, grapes, and forest nuts. What little food they had was not only "insipid," but "sickness was threatened."[376] Modern historian John Mack Faragher observed that, by years end

---

[376] Ranck, *Boonesborough.* 63.

[their] food supply was so low that some of the women followed the cattle around, watching to see what they ate, then boiled the same greens with a piece of salt pork for their families.[377]

Colonel Bowman described in his plea to General Edward Hand of Fort Pitt that, because the Natives "burned all" their "corn" that fall, "many of the families are left desolate...[as] we have no more than two months bread" and "necessity has obliged many of our young men to go to the Monongahale for clothing." Bowman continued in true frontiersman fashion, writing, "We must at any rate suffer."[378] One of his rangers later attested that "he was allowed but one single pint of Corn per day, and that he had to grind it himself of a hand mill...[for] there was nothing else."[379] The garrisons were also devoid of meat and, as Daniel's letter to the Virginian authorities conveyed, the settlers were "destitute of the necessary article of salt."[380]

Salt was more than a staple on the frontier; it was the difference between life and death. It was required for "curing the provisions of the garrison," providing security and a valuable extension in their food supply.[381] Without salt, the

---

[377] Faragher, *Daniel Boone.* 153.

[378] Bowman, John. "Col. John Bowman to General Edward Hand, December 12, 1777," in *Frontier Defense on the Upper Ohio, 1777-1778,* Reuben Gold Thwaits and Louise Phelps Kellogg, eds., Madison: Wisconsin Historical Society, 1912. 183.

[379] Faragher, *Daniel Boone.* 153.

[380] Boone, Daniel. "Petition to the Virginia General Assembly, endorsed November 25, 1777" in *Petitions of the Early Inhabitants of Kentucky to the General Assembly of Virginia, 1769-1792.* James Rood Robertson, ed., (Louisville, Kentucky: John P Morton, 1914), 43.

[381] Faragher, *Daniel Boone.* 154.

settlers were required to hunt nearly every day, exposing themselves and the fort to imminent danger.

The crises reached its height on New Year's Day, 1778, when Daniel agreed to lead a small expedition of about thirty men to the Licking River's lower salt springs. It was a truly bold endeavor, for the fort was under the continually watchful eye of the Native, who "would fall upon them" at any moment "with great ferocity."[382] Laden with large iron kettles to assist the turning of the spring's brine into salt, the small party departed for the Lower Blue Licks on January 8, 1778.

The men worked the spring at a grueling pace in the wretched winter weather, converting eight hundred gallons of brine into one bushel of pure salt.[383] After four weeks, the team sourced several hundred bushels and "dispatched about half of it to the [fort]."[384] Salt making was more than just arduous—it was highly dangerous. Life in the western forest revolved around the salt lick, either for nutrition or for hunting. They were the rest stops of the wilderness and formed the foundation of its complex food chain. Most all game was concentrated around the licks, drawing the white and red hunter alike. One 1769 party witnessed the lick "covered with a moving mass of buffaloes, which [they] … estimated by the … thousands."[385]

Daniel understood that the Natives often frequented the licks, not for the profit of game but of white scalps, so he employed watch parties on their outer perimeters. Although this

---

[382] Abbott, *Daniel Boone.* 191.
[383] These numbers are taken from Lyman Drapers Manuscripts, wherein he credits the 'respectable authority of Joseph Ficklin, who was a youthful defender of Bryan's Station when attacked in 1782.'
[384] Faragher, *Daniel Boone.* 155.
[385] Draper Manuscripts, *Life of Daniel Boone*, 3B:50.

ultimately tempered the party's bounty, Daniel thought it prudent. Most of Boonesborough's able men were concentrated at the lick, leaving their woman and children highly exposed and without defense. If his men were killed, Boonesborough would share the same fate.

Early on Saturday morning, February 7, however, as Daniel was out hunting alone, a party of four braves caught his tracks and soon fell upon him. He immediately tried to cut his nearly four-hundred-pound load of buffalo and escape on his horse, but his knife was frozen in its scabbard. He never cleaned the blood and grease from the blade and it succumbed to the Kentucky frost. After this failed attempt, the braves were nearly at his throat and "an animated chase commenced."[386]

After about a mile, with "bullets [singing] about his ears," Daniel surrendered. One of the bullets had cut loose the strap of his powder horn—he was without defense and twice the age of the young and agile braves. Daniel also knew both the passions and abilities of the Natives and understood the next shot would be "aimed to kill." [387] Suspending his tracks, he hid behind a tree and stood his rifle on the opposite side to signal his submission. Once upon him, the braves laughed, as they immediately recognized the famous hunter and the true victory of their chase.

The braves led their prized catch to their camp near the ancient war trace on Hinkston's Creek. Daniel's eyes were amazed. In the "sheltered part of the valley blazed a fire thirty or forty feet long, and around it sat a party of more than a hundred Shawnee warriors, fully armed."[388] Among the

---

[386] Draper, *The Life of Daniel Boone.* 461.
[387] Bakeless, *Daniel Boone.* 160.
[388] Bakeless, *Daniel Boone.* 160.

warriors Daniel recognized British regulars, masked by their native façade. All faces, red or white, were painted for war.

Daniel immediately discerned that the great party's compass pointed towards Boonesborough and connected that such a party would quickly overwhelm its weak ramparts and inhabitants in a matter of minutes. Boonesborough's fortifications were reportedly in great despair and their people starving, weak, and entirely without defense, as most all of its able men were absent from the fort making salt. Attacked, the settlers would be caught off guard, the fort immediately taken, and the captives tortured and killed. Daniel's deep understanding of the Native's customs and habits, however, served to his advantage.

He was led up to Chief Blackfish—*Cottawamago*— heir of the great Shawnee chief Cornstalk, who Daniel fought nearly twenty years earlier on Braddock's campaign. Three months before, on November 10, Cornstalk was murdered by an American solider while on a mission of peace at Point Pleasant.[389] Blackfish's mission was to avenge his death and Boonesborough was his target. As Virginian Governor Patrick Henry understood, the British leaders at Fort Detroit also took advantage of Blackfish's rage, encouraging the chief to attack the American settlements on the frontier in hopes of repressing the revolutionary American insurgence.

Daniel Boone historian Meredith Mason Brown believed that the British, in assisting the Native's attacks on American frontiersman, sought to advance three objectives: "to reassert control over the Ohio Valley; to hold onto Canada; and to divert American military forces from the coastal colonies."[390]

---

[389] Draper, *The Life of Daniel Boone.* 460.
[390] Brown, *Frontiersman..* 94.

London had explicitly directed Lieutenant Governor Henry Hamilton of Fort Detroit to employ Natives "in making a Diversion and exciting an alarm upon the frontiers of Virginia and Pennsylvania."[391] Hamilton in turn furnished the Natives with guns, ammunition, tomahawks, and war paint—including "eighty pounds of rose pink and five hundred pounds of vermilion."[392] A Virginian woman who lived in Detroit later remembered that "[Hamilton] did all in his Power to induce all Nations of Indians to massacre the Frontier Inhabitants...and paid very high prices in Goods for the Scalps."[393] Hamilton's efforts succeeded, for, in the Declaration of Independence, Thomas Jefferson listed among the "repeated injuries" that King George had brought "upon the Inhabitants of our Frontier, the merciless Indian Savages, whose known Rule of Warfare, is an undistinguished Destruction." Jefferson's letter to Hamilton's superior speaks to the strength of the British's strategic yet unruly position

> The known rule of warfare with the Indian Savages is an indiscriminate butchery of men women and children...[Hamilton] associates small parties of whites under his immediate command with large parties of the Savages, & sends them to act, not against our Forts or

---

[391] Lord Germain to Sir Guy Carleton, White Hall, March 26, 1777, sent to Lieutenant Governor Hamilton from Quebec, May 21, 1777, printed in Consul Willshire Butterfield, *History of the Girtys* (Cincinnati: Robert Clarke & Co. 1890), 342-344.

[392] Ranck, *Boonesborough:* 1.

[393] "Daniel Sullivan to Colonel John Cannon, Fort Pitt, March 20, 1778" in *Frontier Defense on the Upper Ohio 1777-1778*, Reuben Gold Thwaits and Louise P. Kellogg, eds., Madison: State Historical Society of Wisconsin, 1912), 231-232.

armies in the field, but farming settlement on our frontiers.[394]

Although coastal warfare dominated the American Revolution's attention, the British succeeded at sequestering the push of American frontiersman—if only for the moment.

Daniel recognized one Shawnee brave, Captain Will, who captured him nine years before on his first journey into Kentucky, and boldly yelled "How d' do, Captain Will."[395] Captain Will was entirely surprised and the situation's weight relieved. Daniel's open admittance of Captain Will's previous success tempered the moment, as he knew that the Natives admired him and were "invariably pleased on the rare occasions when they outwitted him."[396] Daniel seemed to understand the pride of the Native.

Lyman Draper described the following scene as "most ludicrous," as both Daniel and Blackfish displayed "mock friendship and civility…with all the grace and politeness of which [Daniel] was a master."[397] After their initial pleasantries, Blackfish inquired if Daniel was associated with the salt-makers at the Blue Licks. Seeing no choice, Daniel admitted his allegiance. Although externally calm, his mind racked with stratagem. Daniel knew that, if he could not turn Blackfish's warriors from their vengeful path, not only would he risk the lives of his thirty men, but the lives of every woman and child

[394] Jefferson, Thomas. "Letter to William Phillips, July 22, 1779" in *Calendar of Virginia State Papers and Other Manuscripts,* William R. Palmer, ed., 11 vols. (1875-1893; rpt., New York: Kraus Reprint Corp., 1960-1969), 1:322.

[395] Bakeless, *Daniel Boone.* 162.

[396] Bakeless, *Daniel Boone.* 163.

[397] Draper, *The Life of Daniel Boone.* 463.

in Boonesborough. The Native party outnumbered Daniel's four to one and the advantage of surprise would give additional weight to an already advantaged position. Daniel's understanding of Native nature taught him that the braves needed victory, although the size of such victory was of little import. Thus, Daniel, in a prudent show of finesse, told Blackfish that he would surrender his camp at the Blue Licks as long as "they should not be tortured or forced to run the gauntlet."[398]

The next morning, Daniel led the large Shawnee party to the salt camp where he then convinced his men to surrender. Sixty years later, his speech to the Shawnee on behalf of his men was remembered by one of his fellow salt-makers

> Brothers! You have got all the young men; to kill them, as has been suggested, would displease the Great Spirit, and you could not then expect future success in hunting nor war; and if you spare them they will make you fine warriors, and excellent hunters to kill game for your squaws and children. These young men have done you no harm; they were engaged in a peaceful occupation, and unresistingly surrendered upon my assurance that such a step was the only safe one; I consented to their capitulation on the express condition that they should be made prisoners of war and treated well; I now appeal both to your honor and your humanity; spare them, and the great Spirit will smile upon you.[399]

---

[398] Bakeless, *Daniel Boone.* 164.
[399] Draper, *The Life of Daniel Boone.* 465.

Hearing Daniel's pleas, the Shawnee voted on whether to sacrifice or show mercy to their captives. The ballot ruled sixty-one to fifty-nine for mercy. Daniel's energy, prudence, and sagacity saved the lives of his both his men their families. Daniel's fellow prisoners popularly concluded that, "but for Boone's influence, they all would have been massacred, Boonesborough taken, and its helpless inmates left at the cold mercy of the conquerors."[400] Daniel's plan worked perfectly: the Shawnees' revenge was quelled and their plans abbreviated without the letting of blood. Boonesborough could live for another day.

On their march back to the Shawnee town of Little Chillicothe, Daniel joked and made friends with many of the braves. He understood that the overall success of his efforts would result only from a long game, played with patience and on the Native's terms. This game, however, fooled both the Natives and his own party, and most likely caused suspicion in the latter.

The large party reached the camp that night and Daniel found a large group of braves clearing a pathway in the snow. Although Blackfish promised to not torture Daniel's men, he never promised to spare their leader.

Such a test was to be found in the rigor of the gauntlet. This was a standard practice among many of the Ohio Valley Indian tribes, derived either directly or indirectly from the Ancient Roman practice of the *Fustuarium*, a form of physical punishment where the captive is forced down a row of his peers to be repeatedly beaten with heavy clubs, whips, or anything worth its weight from both sides—sometimes to the death. The

---

[400] Draper, *The Life of Daniel Boone*. 465.

early Hellenistic Greek historian Polybius wrote of such a gauntlet in his work, *The Histories*

> The tribune takes a cudgel and just touches the condemned man with it, after which all in the camp beat or stone him, in most cases dispatching him in the camp itself. But even those who manage to escape are not saved thereby: impossible! For they are not allowed to return to their homes, and none of the family would dare to receive such a man in his house. So that those who have of course fallen into this misfortune are utterly ruined.[401]

For the Shawnee Indians, however, it appears that the purpose of the gauntlet was to test the strength and vigor—or resolve—of their captives. It was to sort the weak from the strong; to peel back the fascia of their foes and glimpse their inner pride—or lack thereof.

Stripped of his shirt, Daniel lined up to run the gauntlet on that cold February night, his men watching fearfully from the side. His many years among the Natives taught him that any deviation in honor would end his life, no matter his captors' respect of his abilities. Staring down the gauntlet, he knew that one step would determine his fate, proving either dignity and honor or death.

Speed was the key. Historically, most captives hesitated, forcing a concentrated beating and eventual, yet slow, death. Daniel would accept nothing but dignity and life—life for himself, his men, and for the families within Boonesborough. Down the dark corridor of over one hundred thirsty braves he

---

[401] *The Histories* 6. 37. 1-4 Loeb ed., 3:353.

would solidify his honor and attain Blackfish's respect. His body burning from the cold, the focal captive erupted from the starting line. With backbreaking speed, Daniel zigzagged back and forth, parleying each blow with a separating movement. When one brave stood in his path, intent on delivering the final blow to end the affair, Daniel, as though a bull charging his prey, "butted him in the chest with his head," knocking the large brave backwards. Victorious, the bloody captive beat the gauntlet.

About a month later, on March 10, Blackfish took the prisoners to Detroit, to collect his pay from the British, "who had encouraged them to go on the warpath."[402] Lieutenant-Governor Hamilton received the Shawnee captives, pitying their helpless state. Immediately, the British commander recognized Daniel and offered one hundred pounds to ransom him. In a to his commanding officer, Governor Hamilton wrote to Sir Guy Carleton on April 5, 1777, "These Shawanesse delivered up four of their prisoners to me; but took Boone with them expecting by his means to affect something."[403]

Blackfish was unmoved by Hamilton's sum, for his plan for Daniel was more important than English silver. Daniel was the key to taking Boonesborough and Boonesborough was the key to taking back the Ohio Valley. Blackfish understood that, if he "could lay [Boonesborough] in ashes, making it the funeral pyre of all its inmates," the "weaker forts" of the Ohio Valley would be "immediately abandoned by their garrisons in despair."[404] Daniel was the key to Boonesborough and Boonesborough was the key to the West.

---

[402] Bakeless, *Daniel Boone. 169-*171.
[403] Lofaro, *Daniel Boone.* 89.
[404] Abbott, *Daniel Boone.* 192.

As soon as Blackfish returned to Little Chillicothe, he began the adoption ceremonies of many of Daniel's men. Daniel was himself transformed from a Captain in the Virginia militia to *Sheltowee*—meaning Big Turtle—a Shawnee warrior. Blackfish adopted *Sheltowee* into his family and treated him as blood of his blood. In fact, most historians conclude that Daniel killed Blackfish's son one-year prior in a skirmish outside of Boonesborough. Perhaps Blackfish's adoption of *Sheltowee* was a result of this connection—blood of his blood.

This honorable hospitality was unique and unexpected, as John C. Abbott concluded, "The Indians seem to have had great respect for Boone." Abbott continued

> Even with them [Daniel] had acquired the reputation of being a just and humane man, while his extraordinary abilities, both as a hunter and a warrior, had won their admiration.[405]

His character was silent but admirable, pensive but courageously formidable. Blackfish hoped in Daniel's full acculturation, perhaps even hopeful of a future chief. In *Sheltowee*, Blackfish saw a warrior and a brother; a leader and a son.

The ceremonies, although painful due to the plucking of hair and extreme washing, yielded a fine-tuned brave, painted and clothed in true Native fashion. *Sheltowee* could scarcely be distinguished from his Native brothers. Both Blackfish and his wife treated Daniel with respect and "addressed him as son," making no "distinction between him and their two real

---

[405] Abbott, *Daniel Boone*. 193.

children."[406] Over the course of the next four months, *Sheltowee* lived, hunted, and communed with his "self-constituted Shawnee kinsmen."[407]

Among Penn's woods, Daniel early learned the Algonquian language of the Delaware, which he invariably used among their grand-nation, the Shawnee.[408] *Sheltowee's* kinship with the Shawnee was so great that many years later his granddaughter met an old Shawnee women at Fort Leavenworth, Kansas, who "beamed when she heard that the white woman talking to her was" *Sheltowee's* kin. The old woman was one of Blackfish's daughters—*Sheltowee's* adopted sisters—and she remembered the great kindness *Sheltowee* had shown her half a century before.[409]

Daniel's acculturation was so complete that some later Boone historians speculate that he even took a Shawnee wife, although there is nothing concrete in these claims. While the absence of evidence is not the evidence of absence, we can positively conclude that Daniel's connection with the Shawnees created "suspicions about his loyalty," which "continued among some of the other adopted salt boilers."[410]

Daniel's own "autobiography" speaks well of his time amongst the Ohio Indians

> I became a son, and had a great share in the affection of my new parents, brothers, sisters, and friends. I was exceedingly familiar and friendly with them, always

---

[406] Bakeless, *Daniel Boone.* 178.
[407] Ranck, *Boonesborough.* 68.
[408] Trowbridge, Charles Christopher. *Shawnese Traditions.* Ann Arbor: *University of Michigan Press, 1939.* 9, 55, 67.
[409] Draper, Lyman. *Draper Manuscripts,* 6S228, 16C28.
[410] Lofaro, *Daniel Boone.* 92.

appearing as cheerful and satisfied as possible, and they put great confidence in me....The Shawanesse king took great notice of me, and treated me with profound respect, and entire friendship, often entrusting me to hunt at my liberty. I frequently returned with the spoils of the woods, and as often presented some of what I had take to him, expressive of duty to my sovereign.[411]

In every sense, the letter on Patrick Henry's desk was correct. Daniel Boone was dead, for *Sheltowee* had killed him.

The Revenant

In early June of 1778, however, Sheltowee "scented the impending danger" of Blackfish's plan to once again attempt to take Boonesborough. By mid-June, he witnessed over four hundred and fifty braves assemble in the Old Chillicothe town. They were painted and dressed for war. With such numbers against the fort and no leader inside its wall to mount a defense, Boonesborough was as good as dead.

Daniel had a decision to make. For the first time in his life, he lived and hunted in nearly perfect peace; he had been accepted and fully adopted into Blackfish's family; and he was not troubled by land titles, commanding officers, American Revolution, or colonial politics. Living within the reciprocity of Nature with the Native, in many ways, was a true representation of his foundational visions of *Kanta-ke*. But his family was in danger.

---

[411] Boone, Daniel. *The Adventures of Colonel Daniel.* 13.

It appears that Daniel's decision had been made months before, for he had secretly stockpiled loads of ammunition and flint outside the purview of the Shawnee for just the occasion.[412] Just as Big Jim killed James and Dragging Canoe killed Captain Twitty, however, Daniel appears to have made the indigenous choice—to protect, defend, and support your own, no matter your destiny's desire or communal allegiance.

While his fellow braves were out on a bear hunt, near modern day Xenia, Ohio, Daniel stayed back with the women and children, attending the fire and camp gear. After he heard the report of rifles, proving the braves' distance from their camp, Daniel unleashed his horse and rode south to Boonesborough.

Daniel rode hard through the night, using the "bed of running streams to obliterate his tracks." The forty-three-year-old woodsman knew that at any moment a party of four hundred and fifty young, fit, ready, and vengeful braves would be upon him. About ten o'clock the next morning his horse gave out, unable to continue. Not losing a moment, Daniel quickly dismounted and continued on foot, breaking his path by following fallen trees.

Daniel covered the expanse of one hundred and sixty miles in less than four days, "eating only one meal besides his jerked venison."[413] Fording the Ohio was no simple task, although it provided a great break of his trail and detached his pursuers in both distance and trajectory. John Bakeless concluded, "[Daniel's] journey was an amazing record of endurance and self-reliance." Although Bakeless's conclusion is not altogether untrue, Daniel's escape and following odyssey

---

[412] Lofaro, *Daniel Boone.* 91.
[413] Bakeless, *Daniel Boone.* 183.

attests to more than Daniel's strength and character. It shows his true soul: one that is supreme in its patience, statesmanlike in its prudence, manic in its passions, and feverishly devoted to family.

Deeply fatigued and "bedraggled," Daniel "limped" into Boonesborough, whose population "greeted him as one just risen from the dead."[414] Although the fugitive's return was celebrated with great elation, Daniel found his family's cabin empty. Rebecca had taken their family back east to her father's cabin on the Yadkin when the fort presumed Daniel was dead. Analogous to the romantic Greek poem of Odysseus and his return to Ithaca, wherein his dog Argos alone recognized him, Daniel received an "unexpected greeting" by his family's old cat, "which had not been found since Rebecca and the children went back to the settlements."[415]

Standing in his empty doorway, he felt dejected and entirely alone. His tired eyes stared at the "rough logs, the cold, blackened fireplace, the empty pegs" and found that, although he had saved both Boonesborough and most his thirty men, he had lost his family.[416] Worst of all, after he risked his life to save Boonesborough the previous winter and then successfully defended it from Blackfish's siege in the coming weeks, he was then court marshaled as a traitor, due to his time among the British at Fort Detroit and the Shawnee at Little Chillicothe. Although Daniel won the trial—in fact, he was so exonerated that they promoted him to the rank of Major—his next journey was the most important of his life.[417]

---

[414] Bakeless, *Daniel Boone.* 184; Ranck, *Boonesborough.* 69.
[415] Lofaro, *Daniel Boone.* 94.
[416] Bakeless, *Daniel Boone.* 185.
[417] Ranck, *Boonesborough.* 105.

Hitherto, Daniel had always pushed westward—forever curiously seeking what lay beyond the next cliff, the next bluff. From his youth, he had dreamed of the pure West, steadied his compass forever toward its sublime sunsets, and incessantly longed for the many mysteries of the lands beyond the mountains. Now was the moment of his life.

In December 1779, he departed the station that bore his name. He went east; east to the Yadkin; east to be with his family.

CHAPTER 8

Ghost of Kenta-ke

The social anthropologist Bronislaw Malinowski argued that myth, "in its living, primitive form" is more than story and folklore, but "a reality lived." Indigenous mythology is both historical and present; it is both dead and entirely living. The story of creation celebrates the work of the Creator, but it also empowers the created. Endowed with the magical lens through which life's rhythm can be perceived, the storyteller occupies the ghostly realm of the dead, the living, and the still to be.

In this muddy mixture, we can at once "celebrate, mourn, and honor" the past, while also anticipate the future, when the "great heroes may return to their people, bearing powerful medicine to restore…glory."[418] And the ghost of our story is still speaking to us.

Toward the end of Henry Clay's life, it is said that the ghost of Daniel Boone haunted him. Attributed to his daughter-in-law, the story appeared in the Louisville *Courier Journal* on August 31, 1884. Shortly "before his last and fatal visit to

---

[418] *American Indian Myths and Legends.* Richard Erdoes & Alfonso Ortiz, ed., New York: Pantheon Books, 1984, xv.

Washington," Clay, a Kentucky Senator and author of the Bluegrass System—the great economic commercialization of Kentucky—was writing in his library at Ashland. A great storm rumbled outside and with a flash of its thunder a "grizzled and weather beaten" figure appeared. Buckskin covered the "unbidden guest's" imposing frame and a six-foot rifle clung to his aged hands.

Although carefully secured and locked tight, Clay's great estate provided no impediment to his guest's will. The hunter entered the library and sat gently across from Clay's writing desk. He stared mournfully at his host. Not a word pierced the silence. Darkness befell the room, as though a heavy winter blanket had been lowered on Clay's soul. After a few short but deafening moments, the thunder clapped and the premonition disappeared. Soon after, the retiring statesman died.[419]

Although entirely speechless, the ghost of Daniel Boone said it all. The same year that Daniel died in Missouri, Henry Clay engineered the territory's statehood. "The People" of Kentucky defeated the people of *Kanta-ke*, and Henry Clay's economic "Bluegrass System" defeated Daniel's Edenic Bluegrass philosophy. Although he died a citizen of the United States, Daniel was, during his lifetime, a subject of both George II and George III of England; a citizen of Transylvania; an adopted brave of the Shawnee; and a subject of both Charles IV of Spain and the Emperor Napoleon of France during his early years in Missouri. He was a man without a country, for the woods were his home.

---

[419] Louisville *Courier Journal* on August 31, 1884.

Daniel's life is a living eulogy of the West's simple purities and sublime beauties. Clay's ghost depicts a story unfinished, or, perhaps, a story without an end. The ghost of *Kanta-ke* is our mythology and it is built on pain and empathy, on nature and the created's power to continually co-create.

. . .

The picture of Daniel Boone is as elusive as the wilderness he chased. Although often considered a representative American man, Daniel's world was the wilderness forever beyond Anglo settlement and his genius was found under its complex, part Indian, part white, but entirely natural canopy.

Daniel often claimed that he had never been lost in the woods—he did admit to being momentarily befuddled on one occasion—yet he was entirely adrift when he came out of it. Robert Morgan noted, "He was at home with trees around him, and animals and stars, and Indians." Where he lost his way, however, was "where the trace became a turnpike, the trail became a street."[420]

After reuniting with his family in 1778, Daniel spent the majority of the next fifteen years in the East. He tried his hand in politics, business, law, land speculation and surveying. He failed in every endeavor and slowly divorced himself from society. Frontier historian Arthur K. Moore observed that, although pioneer heroes such as Daniel Boone were the pivotal characters on the frontier's dynamic stage, once the wilderness

---

[420] Morgan, *Boone: A Biography.* 347.

and its natural inhabitants receded, so also receded civilization's need for its former champions.

Daniel's elusive and unfinished portrait is also plagued with self-defeating irony, as the more it was realized, the more barren its landscape became. Daniel's deep love for the untouched wilderness paved a navigable path for civilization to follow. By 1799, the irony of Daniel's life was plain to him. More than any other single man, Daniel, who sought to peacefully enjoy the boundless bounties of the West, had created a world that repelled his position and razed the foundation of his soul. He was a man who loved the wilderness for its own sake and who found extreme delight in its simple purity, yet he led civilization to destroy it. Robert Morgan concluded

> From the Blue Ridge to the Bluegrass, from the Yadkin to the Yellowstone, no man sought and loved the wilderness with more passion and dedication. Yet none did more to lead settlers and developers to destroy that wilderness in a few short decades. ...Few white men of his time came close to understanding and appreciating the Native Americans as well as Boone did, yet few did as much, ultimately, to displace the Indians and destroy their habitat and culture.[421]

Thirty years after he "discovered" it, *Kanta-ke* was lost. The beavers, deer, bears, turkeys, buffalo, and the Native had been "replaced by lawyers and politicians and crooks."

---

[421] Morgan, *Boone: A Biography.* 429-430.

Although Daniel zealously sought the many mysteries of the West and forever lived according to the silent melody of its undulating rivers and mountains, of its infinite prairies and canopies, the budding American republic found in Daniel's legacy an "icon of curiosity, courage, character, and wonder" but not the deeply philosophical, Indian-like, solitude-loving, and peaceful woodsman of the wilderness that he was at his core.[422]

Richard Slotkin believed that it was the "figure of Daniel Boone" and not Daniel Boone himself "that became the most significant, most emotionally compelling myth-hero of the early republic." This slight distinction in terms begets considerable consequences. Slotkin described this "myth-hero" as a "lover of the spirit of the wilderness," although his "acts of love and sacred affirmation" are instead viewed as "acts of violence against that spirit and her avatars."[423] American politicians and businessmen would use this simple woodsman's legend to encourage militant national expansion, manifest destiny, and the western removal of the Natives from their ancient lands. Simply, the message of the man—his received genius, the emotive force of his actions, the legend of the frontier—precipitates far more for history than the nature and actual substance of the man's life, purpose, and spirit.

The legend of Daniel Boone as the American myth-hero is perhaps best understood in the aftermath of the Battle of New Orleans. In his 1815 address on the House floor, just five years before Daniel's death, Georgia Representative George Troup declared that America's recent victory over the British was due to its reliance on the western yeoman. He declared

---

[422] Morgan, *Boone: A Biography.* 369; 447.
[423] Slotkin, *Regeneration Through Violence.* 21-22.

It was the yeomanry of the country marching to the defense of the City of Orleans, the farmers of the country triumphantly victorious over the conquerors of Europe. I came, I saw, I conquered, says the American Husbandman, fresh from his plough.[424]

Troup praised the natural husbandry of the American West as the ultimate protector and defender of the American republic. He praised the toil-hardened naturalness of the plough as the ultimate protector of Liberty's Regime. His phrase, "fresh from his plough," suggests a connective and intimate relationship between the plough and victory—between a cultivated nature and America's triumph.

In Charles A. Goodrich's *History of the United States of America,* "the most widely used textbook in America's secondary schools before the Civil War," he concluded that the perfect balance of the American yeoman's "social virtues" amidst their "primitive purity" led to the realization of their success.[425] The American West may not have had the manufactured splendor of society but it possessed a natural compound that the East lacked: pure and un-indoctrinated freedom. Therefore, America's early republic needed a hero, and the legend of Daniel Boone fit the bill.

Daniel's first biographer, whose book was the most widely read frontier epic of antebellum America, presented Daniel as the "Achilles of the West," for the great hunter "had

---

[424] Georgian House of Representative Mr. Troup delivered address on the House Floor, printed by 'National Intelligencer,' February 17, 1815.
[425] Ward, John William. *Andrew Jackson—Symbol for an Age.* London: Oxford University Press, 1953. 37; Goodrich, Charles A. *History of the United States of America.* New York: 1829. 399.

won [the garden of the earth] from the domination of the savage tribes."[426] The American republic needed a champion to lead the western charge into the land of opportunity. In his work, *The Frontier Mind,* Moore argued that the fledgling republic required a myth-hero to "put a happy face on a matter which somewhat troubled" its "conscience" and its imagination "seized" the modest hunter "as a much-needed symbol and cloaked him with appropriate legends."[427]

The early-nineteenth-century journalist and explorer Charles Wilkins Webber described the imaginary Boone as the "Romulus of Saxon blood," for "he was founding a new empire." Webber continued, writing that the American Romulus "was fed, not upon the wolf's milk—but upon the abundance of mild and serene nature—upon the delicious esculence of her forest game, and fruits of her wild luxuriant vines."[428] Simply, Daniel's legend and not Daniel's history became the civilizing agent in a world that appeared entirely uncivilized and served as a false beacon of hope for America's unseasoned western migration.

Daniel Boone—The Common Man

In her book, *Frontiersman: Daniel Boone and the Making of America,* Meredith Mason Brown wrote, "Boone did not go to hunt in Kentucky to fulfill a lifelong objective of opening up new territory for white settlement." Rather, he

---

[426] Flint, *Biographical Memoir of Daniel Boone.* 227.

[427] Moore, Arthur K. *The Frontier Mind.* Lexington: University of Kentucky Press, 1957. 148.

[428] Webber, Charles Wilkins. *The Hunter-naturalist: Romance of Sporting Or, Wild Scenes and Wild Hunters.* 1852. 171.

"wanted to go…because…the land was rich and the wild game plentiful."[429] A woodsman-philosopher, Daniel felt an ancient connection with the land and animals, a sacred bond of kinship—one shared by his Native brothers. From his youth in Penn's woods, Daniel viewed the wilderness through the Native's eyes.

Michael Lofaro described Daniel's life as full of "irony and ambiguity." In the preface to his magnificent biography of Daniel Boone, Lofaro wrote

> Although remembered and enshrined for his role as a pioneer, he often was happiest following the same wilderness life as Native Americans. With them Daniel was comfortable and familiar, coexisting far more in mutual respect than in warfare. As someone who bridged and understood both native and pioneer cultures, Boone sought to avoid bloodshed, to negotiate solutions to conflicts, and literally to hold on to a shrinking geographical and cultural middle ground as the violence of native-settler conflict and of the Revolutionary War in the West escalated around him in Kentucky.

Unlike the majority of his fellow hunters and pioneers, Daniel's story is one of peace with the Natives, forever seeking to understand and mimic their ways, customs, and philosophies. His contemporaries considered him a white-Indian and the Natives called him their white-brother. The wood's inhabitants were his hunting companions, teachers, and friends, even though they killed two of his sons, pushed his nerves to their

---

[429] Brown, *Frontiersman.* 39.

limits, recurrently stalled his dreams, and forced his family into ruin and bankruptcy.

Before his death, Daniel surprised one visitor, remarking that "I never killed but three [Indians]," for "they have always been kinder to me than whites."[430] Perhaps, however, this irony says it all; Daniel's admiration of the Native—their communal society, formed by honor, respect, strength, and family—sprouted from his great love of the wilderness, its purity, and its natural regime; maybe Daniel understood the true sagacity of the Native in comparison to and in formation with the unfolding American mind, for he communed with both George Washington and Blackfish, Thomas Jefferson and Oconostata.

Kenneth Rexroth wrote in his *Revisited* history of the American West, "Our memory of the Indians connects us with the soil and the waters and the nonhuman life about us," for our "reason and order…can penetrate" their "savage environment," but it "cannot control" it.[431] The story of Daniel Boone is the story of his too slow understanding of the limits of civilization upon the truly abundant world of the Native. In his later life, Daniel appears to have understood the limits of the American mind and believed that, although the American man can penetrate the wilderness, ultimate control was forever beyond his reach; that, although the West was a land of open opportunity, it was also a land called home.

Daniel's affection for the Natives depicted the duality of his nature and his admiration of their ways evidenced the difference of his soul from other American settlers. Later,

---

[430] Wallis, Michael. *The Real Wild West: The 101 Ranch and the Creation of the American West.* New York: St. Martin's Press, 1999. 14.
[431] Rexroth, Kenneth, Classics Revisited LXI: Parkman's History.

Daniel wrote that, "while he could never with safety repose confidence in a Yankee, he had never been deceived by an Indian," and, if he was ever forced to decide, "he should certainly prefer a state of nature to a state of civilization."[432]

Home

In late 1799, Daniel moved his family further west and established his final home on the banks of the great Missouri River. His tenure in the East was complete. Stationed in the Femme Osage Creek Valley, the nearly seventy-year-old woodsman hunted and explored the wilderness beyond Kentucky—the great mountains and prairies, the infinite rivers and boundless horizons. With Derry Coburn and others, he explored the Rocky Mountains and the seemingly boundless prairies before and beyond its great peaks. Some historians suggest that he made it as far as modern day Yellowstone National Park or even the Pacific Ocean. Once again, he was alone in the wilderness; once again he was swaddled by the Native's world.

During his quiet evening of life on the Missouri the aged woodsman's search of solitude increased, as he was singed by the "corruptions and indignities of the world."[433] He was humble and meek, yet still full of life. As the Reverend James E. Welch recorded after his visit in 1818, Daniel exhibited a "very mild countenance, fair complexion, soft and quiet in his manners, but little to say unless spoken to." Welch continued, writing that the aged woodsman was very "fond of quiet

---

[432] Faragher, *Daniel Boone*. 300.
[433] Morgan, *Boone: A Biography*. 430.

retirement, of cool self-possession, and indomitable perseverance."[434] Daniel's family later noted that, upon sight of an approaching visitor, he would often shuffle out of the back door to evade confrontation or conversation and hide in the solace of the woods. On occasion, he would remove himself into the forest for no reason at all. Equipped with only a bearskin, he would lay under the shade of the distant forest singing happily to himself. As his eyesight declined, Rebecca carried his rifle into the woods for him and helped him mark. He also greatly enjoyed the "society of his children and grandchildren," who "delighted in his conversation and rejoiced in every little service of kindness they could render him."[435] During this time of self-reflection, Daniel admitted, "Many heroic actions and chivalrous adventures are related of me which exist only in the region of fancy. With me the world has taken many liberties," although "I have been but a common man."[436]

Daniel only twice returned to Kentucky. It was during his last visit that, "with characteristic simplicity and directness," he visited every man he owed money to and paid the "sum that each man said was due." Tradition has it that, on returning to Missouri, Daniel had but a half a dollar left.[437] Early Boone historian John Mason Peck, who interviewed Daniel shortly before his death, recorded the woodsman's conscience upon his final return

> Now I am ready and willing to die. I am relieved from a
> burden that has long oppressed me. I have paid all my

---

[434] Thwaits, *Daniel Boone*. 237.

[435] Bogart, *Daniel Boone and the Hunters of Kentucky*. 379.

[436] Roche, George. *The Book of Heroes: Great Men and Women in American History*. volume 1. Washington: Regnery Publishing, Inc. 73.

[437] Bakeless, *Daniel Boone*. 406.

debts, and no one will say, when I am gone, "Boone was a dishonest man." I am perfectly willing to die.[438]

His "death song" was now prepared and his honor solidified.

During the late summer of 1820, Daniel experienced frequent bouts of fever. Expecting the worst, his family called Dr. Jones, "who prescribed medications," although Daniel said he "would take nothing," for "he was about worn out."[439] The tired woodsman had spent the majority of the past seventy years in the wilderness, subsisting on nothing more than forest nuts, roots, and fresh game. He often wintered without a fire, so as not to attract unwanted or dangerous guests. He was born in Pennsylvania, yet explored as far west as the Pacific and as far south as modern day Orlando, Florida. Although he was awarded over ten thousand acres over his lifetime, he died without a penny to his name or land enough to bury his rotting remains, as he never understood how to properly file a land claim. He had eleven children, although he survived all but two of them. He was a man of the wilderness—he was a son of nature—and nature was calling.

Daniel knew his time was near. He traveled to the home of his youngest son, Nathan Boone, where he knew he could die in peace near the grave of his beloved Rebecca. Upon his arrival, he asked for his coffin and "thumped at it with his cane to test its soundness." He discussed that he was to be buried next to Rebecca "on the hill by Tuque Creek," which overlooked the great Missouri River's bottom lands.[440] The following morning,

---

[438] Kelsey, D. M. *History of Our Wild West and Stories of Pioneer Life.* Chicago: Thompson & Thomas, 1901. 47
[439] Faragher, *Daniel Boone.* 318.
[440] Faragher, *Daniel Boone.* 318.

the tired woodsman inquired for a bowl of warm milk and for everyone to gather. Seated in the front room of his son's home, with Jemima and Nathan holding his hands, his weary soul accepted his death's song a month before his eighty-sixth birthday. His last words were those of a man at peace: "I am going; don't grieve for me," for "my time has come."

Just before the sunrise crested the eastern horizon on September 26, 1820, Daniel Boone receded into the West.

Conclusions

Daniel's ghost mythology is perhaps best realized in his grave—or lack of grave. In 1845, the Kentucky Legislature passed a resolution to bring the bones of their great founder back to Kentucky. On Saturday September 13, 1845, a large crowd assembled in the streets of Frankfort to observe the delayed triumph of their founder. His revised gravesite overlooked the Kentucky River and a great monolith was placed above his new pine coffin. In 1983, however, speculation arose that the great hunter and woodsman was not actually buried in Frankfort. After exhuming his body, the forensic anthropologist Dr. David Wolf concluded that the body under the Frankfort monument was most likely the remains of a young black man and not the bones of Kentucky's founder. "We say the remains are here," affirms the record keeper at the cemetery, "but who can say what lies beneath the Boone monument in Frankfort?"[441]

Daniel Boone was not the first to settle Kentucky; he was not civilization's epic pathfinder; he was not Kentucky's founder; and he was not an Indian-killer. The monument in

---

[441] Faragher, *Daniel Boone*. 362.

Frankfort today overlooks the dome of Kentucky's capitol, whereas Daniel's lonely grave in Missouri next to his wife overlooks the land of his children and in the mixed community of Anglo-Native culture. Like his lost grave, the true history of Daniel Boone is yet unknown. It is only by the living portrait of his life—by finding him in his woods, with his own gun, and with his own mind—that we can uncover the unfinished mythology of this humble, simple, and "common" woodsman.

Although he loved the Native, Daniel put his family first, and although the Native adopted him as their brother and son, his epic led to the destruction of their land's fertility, purity, and their native identities. It took two centuries for Europeans to destroy the pristine habitat that the Native had cultivated for twenty millennia, and Daniel's path was the trace followed by the steady stream of American debauchery.

Eighteen years after Daniel's death, Andrew Jackson removed his Cherokee brothers from their homelands in what became known as the great "Trail of Tears." The Shawnee were dispersed and their identities dissipated, and Daniel's quiet and peaceful backwoods paradise transformed into the central mercantile enterprise of the young country.[442]

Perhaps, this empathic and painful irony is the answer. The further Daniel ventured into the American West, the more distant he became with the forming American mind and the more connected he became with the Native. Perhaps, his path's failure to sustain his true legacy proves the maxim that the advancing American regime could not contain both *Sheltowee* and Daniel Boone. Perhaps Daniel was not the representative

---

[442] Stephen Aaron's book, *How the West was Lost: The Transformation of Kentucky from Daniel Boone to Henry Clay* largely speaks to this last point.

American man that history has so remembered and he was neither to build an empire nor philosophize on the primitive.

Perhaps he was just a man. The night of Daniel's passing, the *Kanta-ke* sky grew dark. Positioned under its ashen canopy, the braves of Little Chillicothe buried their tomahawks one by one and passed their peace pipes. Their aged chief, Blackfish—*Cottawamago*—walked alone to the edge of their village. In his fight to secure the land of his people and the reciprocity of its abundance, Blackfish had lost many good warriors, but that battle was now over. In the silence that only dusk can bring, he remembered the words of his adopted son, Tecumseh, "Sing your death song and die like a hero going home." Looking up, *Cottawamago* welcomed the spirit of his lost brother, for he and *Sheltowee* were home at last.

Bibliography

"Daniel Sullivan to Colonel John Cannon, Fort Pitt, March 20, 1778" in *Frontier Defense on the Upper Ohio 1777-1778*, Reuben Gold Thwaits and Louise P. Kellogg, eds., Madison: State Historical Society of Wisconsin, 1912).

"Governor Patrick Henry to Colonel William Fleming, February 19th, 1778," in *Frontier Defense On The Upper Ohio, 1777-1778*, Reuben Gold Thwaits, Louise Phelps Kellogg, eds., Madison: Wisconsin Historical Society, 1912.

"Governor Patrick Henry to General Edward Hand, July 27th, 1777," in *Frontier Defense On The Upper Ohio, 1777-1778*, Reuben Gold Thwaits, Louise Phelps Kellogg, eds., Madison: Wisconsin Historical Society, 1912.

"Museum of Native American Artifacts-MISSISSIPPIAN PERIOD 900 AD - 1450 AD". Retrieved 2010-07-18.

A History of Rowan County, North Carolina, Containing Sketches of Prominent Families and Distinguished Men (Salisbury, N.C.: J. J. Bruner, 1881).

Abbott, John S. *Daniel Boone: The Pioneer of Kentucky.* New York: Dodd, Mead & Company, 1874. 42-43.

Aberth, John. *The First Horseman: Disease in Human History.* Pearson-Prentice Hall, 2007.
Adair, James. *The History of the American Indians.* Kathryn E. Holland Braund, ed., Tuscaloosa: The University of Alabama Press, 2005.

Alexis de Tocqueville. *Democracy in America.* trans., ed., Harvey C. Mansfield. Chicago: The University of Chicago Press, 2000.

American Indian Myths and Legends. Richard Erdoes & Alfonso Ortiz, ed., New York: Pantheon Books, 1984.

Arnow, Harriette Simpson, *Seedtime on the Cumberland.* New York, 1960.

Bancroft, George. "History of the United States from the Discovery of the American Continent, Volume 1." Oxford: Oxford University, 1854.

Bancroft, George. *History of the Colonization of United States*. Boston: Charles C Little and James Brown, 1841.

Belue, Ted Franklin, *The Long Hunt: Death of the Buffalo east of the Mississippi*. Mechanicsburg: Stackpole Books 1996.

Bernard Bailyn, *The Peopling of British North America: An Introduction* (New York: Vintage Books, 1986).

Billington, Ray. *Frederick Jackson Turner Historian, Scholar, Teacher* (New York: Oxford University Press, 1973).

Bogart, William Henry. *Daniel Boone and the Hunters of Kentucky*. Boston: Lee and Shepard, 1875.

Bogart, William Henry. *Daniel Boone and the Hunters of Kentucky*. Boston: Lee and Shepard, 1875.

Boome, William P. "Letter from William P. Boone to Lyman Draper, April 27, 1846" in *Draper Manuscripts* 19C1; Lyman Draper interview with Isaiah Boone, 1846, *Draper Manuscripts* 19C61.s

Boone, Daniel. "Petition to the Virginia General Assembly, endorsed November 25, 1777" in *Petitions of the Early Inhabitants of Kentucky to the General Assembly of Virginia, 1769-1792*. James Rood Robertson, ed., (Louisville, Kentucky: John P Morton, 1914).

Boone, Daniel. *Memorial to the Kentucky Legislature*. 1812.

Boone, Daniel. *The Adventures of Colonel Daniel Boone, Formerly a Hunter; Containing a Narrative of the Wars of Kentucky, as Given by Himself.*

Boone, Nathan. *My Father, Daniel Boone: The Draper Interviews with Nathan Boone*. Neal O. Hammon, ed. Lexington: University Press of Kentucky, 1999.

Boorstin, Daniel. *The Lost World of Thomas Jefferson*, Chicago: University of Chicago Press, 1948.

Bowman, John. "Col. John Bowman to General Edward Hand, December 12, 1777," in *Frontier Defense on the Upper Ohio, 1777-1778*, Reuben Gold Thwaits and Louise Phelps Kellogg, eds., Madison: Wisconsin Historical Society, 1912.

Brown, Meredith Mason. *Frontiersman: Daniel Boone and the Making of America*. Baton Rouge: Louisiana State University Press, 2008.

Brown, Meredith Mason. *Frontiersman: Daniel Boone and the Making of America.* Baton Rouge: Louisiana States Universtiy Press, 2008.

Brown, Meredith. *Frontiersman: Daniel Boone and the Making of America.* Baton Rouge: Louisiana States Universtiy Press, 2008.

Callender, Charles, "Shawnee," in Bruce G. Trigger, ed., *Handbook of North American Indians*, 20 vols. (Washington, D., 1978).

Catlin, George, *Letters and Notes on the Manners, Customs, and Conditions of the North American Indians.* New York: Dover Publications, Inc., 1973.

Christopher Gist's Journals, ed. William M. Darlingotn (Pittsburgh, 1893).

Churchill, Winston. *Marlborough: His Life and Times, Book One.* Chicago: Chicago University Press, 1993.

Clough, Elizabeth Thatcher, ed., "Abraham Thomas: 'This Small Legacy of Experience'," *Kentucky Ancestors 26* (Autumn 1990).

Colden, Cadwallader. *The History of the Five Indian Nations of Canada*, 1727.

Collins, Lewis. *History of Kentucky*, 1877. vol ii.

Cook, Noble David. *Born To Die.* Cambridge: Cambridge University Press, 1998.

Daniel Boone Bryan to Draper, Feb. 27, 1843, Draper Manuscripts 22C5.

Denevan, William M. "The Pristine Myth: The Landscape of the Americas in 1492," in *Annals of the Association of American Geographers*, Vol. 82, No. 3. Oxfordshire: Taylor & Francis, Ltd., 1992.

Diamanti, Melissa 1998. *Archaeological Reconnaissance of Ohio River Island National Wildlife Refuge in Pennsylvania, West Virginian and Kentucky and Phase I Archaeological Survey of Manchester Island No. 2, Kentucky.* Report submitted to the U. S. Fish and Wildlife Service, Region 5, Hadley, Ma.

Diary of David McClure, Doctor of Divinity, 1748-1820 (New York: Knickerbocker Press, 1899).

Draper, Lyman C. *The Life of Daniel Boone.* Ted Franklin Belue, ed. Mechanicsburg: Stackpole Books, 1998.

Draper, Lyman, *Manuscripts*, 3B:50.

Draper, Lyman. "Sketches from Border Life," Draper MSS, 27CC33.

Draper, Lyman. *Draper Manuscripts,* 6S228, 16C28.

Draper, Lyman. *Lyman Draper's Manuscripts,* 4B118-ED, 125-Ed.

Dunn, Richard and Dunn, Mary Maples, "Letter from William Penn to the King of the Indians," in The Papers of William Penn, 5 vols. (Philadelphia: University of Pennsylvania Press, 1981-86).

Edmunds, R. David. *Tecumseh and the Quest for Indian Leadership.* 2nd Edition, Mark C Carnes, ed., New York: Person Longman, 2007.

Ellis, Joseph J. *His Excellency, George Washington.* New York: Vintage Books, 2004.

Emerson, Ralph Waldo. "Nature" in *Selected Essays, Lectures, and Poems.* Robert D. Richardson Jr., ed. New York: Bantam Dell, 1990.

Enoch, Harry G. *Pioneer Voices: Interviews with Early Settlers of Clark County Kentucky.*

Etulain, Richard W. "Introduction: The Rise of Western Historiography," in *Writing Western History: Essays on Major Western Historians.* ed., Richard W. Etulain. Albuquerque: University of New Mexico Press, 1991.

Etulain, Richard W. "Introduction: The Rise of Western Historiography," in *Writing Western History: Essays on Major Western Historians.* ed., Richard W. Etulain. Albuquerque: University of New Mexico Press, 1991.

Faragher, John Mack. *Daniel Boone: the Life and Legend of an American Pioneer.* New York: Henry Hold and Company, 1992.

Fischer, David Hacket, *Albion's Seed: Four British Folkways in America.* New York: Oxford University Press, 1989.

Flint, Timothy, *Biographical Memoir of Daniel Boone,* ed. James K Folsom. New Haven: Yale University Press, 1967.

Fox, George. *A Journal of the Life, Travels, Sufferings, Christian Experiences, and Labour of Love of George Fox.* William Armistad, ed. Glascow: W.G. Balckie & Co.

Franklin B. Dexter, ed., *Diary of David McClure, Doctor of Divinity, 1748-1820* (New York, 1899).

Franklin, Benjamin. *Autobiography.* Barns & Co. Inc., 1944.

Franklin, Benjamin. *Ohio Settlement,* London, 1772.

5

Frontier and Section: Selected Essays of Frederick Jackson Turner. ed., Ray Allen Billington. (Englewood Cliffs, N.J.: Prentice-Hall, 1961).

General Kane's *Military History of Great Britain;* Lofaro, Michael A. *Daniel Boone: An American Life.* Lexington: University Press of Kentucky, 2003.

Georgian House of Representative Mr. Troup delivered address on the House Floor, printed by 'National Intelligencer,' February 17, 1815.

Greenspan, Ezra, ed. *Walt Whitman's "Song of Myself": A Sourcebook and Critical Edition.* New York: Routledge, 2005.

Hagy, James William. "The First Attempt to Settle Kentucky: Boone in Virginia," Filson Club Historical Quarterly 53 (July 1979).

Hanna, Charles A. *The Wilderness Trail: The Ventures and Adventurers of the Pennsylvania Traders on the Allegheny Path.* New York: The Knickerbocker Press, 1911.

Harrison, Lowell H., Dawson Nelson L. *A Kentucky Sampler: Essays from The Filson Club History Quarterly 1926—1976.* University Press of Kentucky, 1977.

Haywood, John. *The Civil and Political History of the State of Tennessee* (Knoxville: Heiskell and Brosn, 1803).

Haywood, John. *The Civil and Political History of the State of Tennessee* (Knoxville: Heiskell and Brosn, 1803).

Henderson, Archibald. *The Star of Empire: Phases of the Western Movement in the Old Southwest.* Durham: The Seeman Printery, 1919.

Henderson, Richard. "Judge Richard Henderson's Journal of a Trip to 'Cantuckey' and of Events at Boonesborough in 1775," in Ranck, George Washington, *Boonesborough: Its Founding, Pioneer Struggles, Indian Experiences, Transylvania Days, and Revolutionary Annals.* Louisville: John P. Morton & Company, 1901.

Henderson, Richard. "Letter of Judge Henderson (June 12, 1775) to Proprietors Remaining in North Carolina," in *Boonesborough; Its Founding, Pioneer Struggles, Indian Experiences, Transylvania Days, and Revolutionary Annals,* by George Washington Ranck.
Holmes, Steven (1999). *The Young John Muir: An Environmental Biography.* Madison: Univ. of Wisconsin Press.

6

Houston, Peter. *A Sketch of the Life and Character of Daniel Boone.* Ted Franklin Belue, ed. Mechanicsburg: Stackple Books, 1997.

Hurt, R. Douglas. *The Ohio Frontier: Crucible of the Old Northwest, 1720-1830.* Bloomington: Indiana University Press, 1996.

Jackson Independent Patriot, Nov. 8, 1826.

Jean R. Soderlund, ed., *William Penn and the Founding of Pennsylvania, 1680-1684* (Philadelphia: University of Pennsylvania Press, 1983).

Jefferson, Thomas. "Letter to William Phillips, July 22, 1779" in *Calendar of Virgnia State Papers and Other Manuscripts,* William R. Palmer, ed., 11 vols. (1875-1893; rpt., New York: Kraus Reprint Corp., 1960-1969).

Jefferson, Thomas. "Query XI" in *The Portable Thomas Jefferson.* Merrill Peterson, ed., New York: Penguin Books, 1977.

Jenny Leading Cloud. *American Indian Myths and Legends.* Richard Erdoes & Alfonso Ortiz, ed., New York: Pantheon Books, 1984.

John Dane, "A Declaration of Remarkabell Prouidenses in the Corse of My Lyfe," NEHGR 8 (1854).

John Locke, *Two Treatises of Government*, Peter Laslett, ed., Cambridge Texts in the History of Ideas, Cambridge, 1988, Treatise II.

John Winthrop, "A Modell of Christian Charity Written on Board the Arrabella on the Atlantick Ocean," *Winthrop Papers,* II.

Johnson, J. Stoddard. ed., *First Explorations of Kentucky: Journals of Dr. Thomas Walker, 1750, and Christopher Gist, 1751* (Louisville, 1898).

Johnson, W.C. 1981. *The Campbell Farm Site (36FA26) and Monongahela: A Preliminary Examination and Assessment.* Paper presented at the Fourth Monongahela Symposium, State College, Pennsylvania.

Jonathan Dickinson to Cousin, 17 Oct 1719, Jonathan Dickinson Letterbook, 1715-21, HSP.
Joseph Doddridge, *Notes on the Settlement and Indian Wars of the Western Parts of Virginia and Pennsylvania from 1763-1783 inclusive, Together with a Review of the State of Society and Manners of the First Settlers of the Western Country.* Pittsburgh, 1824.

Journals of Lewis and Clark, Frank Bergon, ed., New York: Penguin Group, 1989.

Kelsey, D. M. *History of Our Wild West and Stories of Pioneer Life.* Chicago: Thompson & Thomas, 1901.

Kolodny, Annette. *The Land Before Her: Fantasy and Experience of the American Frontiers, 1630-1860.* Chapel Hill: The University of North Carolina Press, 1984.

Kroeber, Aldred Louis. *Cultural and Natural Areas of Native North America.* Berkeley: University Of California Press, 1963.

Lawson, John. *History of North Carolina.* Charlotte: Observer Printing House, 1903.

Lepper, T. Bradley. *Ohio Archeology: An Illustrated Chronicle of Ohio's Ancient American Indian Cultures.* Wilmington: Orange Frazer Press, 2005.

Lewis, Jon E. *The Mammoth Book of The West: The Making of the American West.* New York: Carroll & Graf Publishers, Inc., 1996.

Limerick, Patricia Nelson. *Legacy of Conquest: The Unbroken Past of The American West.* New York: W.W. Norton & Company, 1987.

Lofaro, Michael A, *Daniel Boone: An American Life.* University of Kentucky Press, 2003.

Lord Germain to Sir Guy Carleton, White Hall, March 26, 1777, sent to Lieutenant Governor Hamilton from Quebec, May 21, 1777, printed in Consul Willshire Butterfield, *History of the Girtys* (Cincinnati: Robert Clarke & Co. 1890).

Lord, Lewis. "How Many People Were Here Before Columbus?" in *The U.S. News & World Report,* 1997.

Lucien Beckner, ed., "Reverend John D. Shane's Interview with Pioneer William Clinkenbeard," *FCHQ* 2 (April 1928).

Lyman Draper interview with Edward Byram, October 2, 1863, *Draper Manuscripts* 19S170.

Lyman Draper interview with Peter Smith, 1863, *Draper Manuscripts* 18S113.

Madison, James, "Property," in *50 Core American Documents.*

Mann, Charles, C. *1491: New Revelations of the America Before Columbus.* New York: Vintage Books: 2005.

McClure, David, *Diary of David McClure*. New York: The Knickerbocker Press, 1899.

McNeill, William H, *Plagues and Peoples*. Garden City: Anchor Press, 1976.

Miller, Randall M., Pencak, William A., eds. *Pennsylvania: A History of the Commonwealth*. Penn State University Press; 1 edition (October 22, 2002).

Moize, Elizabeth A. *Daniel Boone, First Hero of the Frontier*. 1895.

Moore, Arthur K. *The Frontier Mind*. Lexington: University of Kentucky Press, 1957.

Morgan, Edmund S. *American Heroes: Profiles of Men and Women who Shaped Early America*. New York: W.W. Norton & Company, 2010.

Morgan, Robert. *Boone: A Biography*. Chapel Hill: Algonaquin Books of Chapel Hill, 2007. Niles' Register, X, 361 (June 15, 1816).

Muir, John, "Save the Redwoods," in *John Muir: Nature Writings*. William Cronon, ed., New York: Library of America, 1997.

Muir, John, "The American Forests," in *John Muir: Nature Writings*. William Cronon, ed., New York: Library of America, 1997.

Nestor, James. *Breath, The New Science of a Lost Art*. New York: Riverhead Books, 2020.

Noble, David W. "Frederick Jackson Turner: The Machine and the Loss of the Covenant" in *Historians Against History: The Frontier Thesis and the National Covenant in American Historical Writing since 1830*. Minneapolis: University of Minnesota Press, 1965.

O'Brien, Michael, I. *Irish Pioneers in Kentucky*. CreateSpace Independent Publishing Platform, 2014.

Peck, John Mason. "Life of Daniel Boone, The Pioneer of Kentucky" in *Makers of American History*. New York: The University Society, 1904.

Penn, William, "For of Light Came Sight," in *The Quaker Reader*, Wallingford: Pendle Hill Publications, 1962.

Penn, William. Letter to the "King of the Indians," October 18, 1681, Richard Dunn and Mary Maples Dunn, eds., *The Papers of William Penn*, 5 vols. (Philadelphia: University of Pennsylvania Press, 1981-86).

9

Perkins, James H. *North American Review*, LXII, (January, 1846).

Pierson, George Wilson. "The Frontier and American Institutions: A Criticism of the Turner Theory," in *The Turner Thesis: Concerning the Role of the Frontier in American History.* ed., George Rogers Taylor. Lexington: D. C. Heath and Company, 1972.

Punke, Michael. *The Revenant.* New York: Picador Publishing, 2002.

Ranck, George Washington. *Boonesborough: Its Founding, Pioneer Struggles, Indian Experiences, Transylvania Days, and Revolutionary Annals.* Louisville: John P. Morton & Company, 1901.

Reverend F. L. Hanks' lecture before the New York Historical Society, December 1852.
Rexroth, Kenneth, Classics Revisited LXI: Parkman's History.

Rice, Otis. *Frontier Kentucky*, University Press of Kentucky: Second Edition (July 20, 1993).

Richter, Daniel K. *The Ordeal of the Long-House: The Peoples of the Iroquois League in the Era of European Colonization* (Chapil Hill, 1992).

Henderson, Gwynn A., Jobe, Cynthia E., & Turnbow, Christopher A., *Indian Occupation and Use in Northern and Eastern Kentucky during the Contact Period (1540-1795): An Initial Investigation* (Frankfort, 1986).

Robert A Genheimer, ed., "Cultures Before Contact: The Late Prehistory of Ohio and Surrounding Regions" in *Ohio Archaeological Council*, 2000.

Robert Orme, "Journal of General Braddock's Expedition," British Library.

Ward, Matthew. *Breaking The Backcountry: The Seven Years' War In Virginia And Pennsylvania 1754-1765,* University of Pittsburgh Press; 1 edition (October 17, 2004).

Robin Wall Kimmerer, "Learning the Grammar of Animacy," in *Colors of Nature: Culture, Identity, and the Natural World.* Alison H Deming & Lauret E. Savor, ed., Minneapolis: Milkweed Editions, 2011.

Roche, George. *The Book of Heroes: Great Men and Women in American History.* volume 1. Washington: Regnery Publishing, Inc.

Shetler, Stanwyn. "Three faces of Eden," *In Seeds of change: A Quincentennial Commemoration,* ed. H. J. Viola and C. Margolis. Washington: Smithsonian Institution Press, 1997.

Slotkin, Richard. *Regeneration Through Violence: The Mythology of the American Frontier, 1600-1860.* Norman: University of Oklahoma Press, 1973.

Smith, Adam. *An Inquiry into the Nature and Causes of the Wealth of Nations.* Edwin Cannan, ed. Chicago: University of Chicago Press, 1976. Book 1, Chapter 5.

Smith, Henry Nash. *Virgin Land: The American West as a Symbol and Myth.* Cambridge: Harvard University Press, 1950.

Smith, James. "Col. James Smith's Life Among the Delawares, 1755-1759" in *The Account of Mary Rowlandson and Other Indian Captivity Narratives.* Horace Kephart, ed. Mineola: Dover Publications, 1915.

Strauss, Leo. *Natural Right and History.* Chicago: University of Chicago Press, 1953.
The Histories 6. 37. 1-4 Loeb ed., 3:353.

The Papers of Thomas Jefferson, vol. 40, *4 March–10 July 1803*, ed. Barbara B. Oberg. Princeton: Princeton University Press, 2013.

Thomas J. Farnham, *Travels in the Great Western Prairies, the Anahuac and Rocky Mountains, and in the Oregon Territory* (Poughkeepsie, N. Y., 1841).

Timberlake, Henry. *The Memoirs of Lt. Henry Timberlake: The Story of a Soldier, Adventurer, and Emissary to the Cherokees, 1756-1765.* Duane H. King, ed., Cherokee: Cherokee Indian Press, 2007.

Tindall, George Brown and Shi, David E, "Settling The Middle Colonies and Georgia," *in America, A Narrative History* (New York: W. W. Norton & Company, 2004), Volume I.

Trowbridge, Charles Christopher. *Shawnese Traditions.* Ann Arbor: University of Michigan Press, 1939.

Turner, Frederick Jackson. "Contributions of the West to American Democracy," in *Frontier in American History*.

Turner, Frederick Jackson. "Hunter Type," in Jacobs, ed., *Frederick Jackson Turner's Legacy*.

Turner, Frederick Jackson. "Problems in American History," *The Aegis*, November 4, 1892, repr. in *Early Writings*.

Turner, Frederick Jackson. *Rise of the New West: 1819-1829* (New York: Harper and Brothers, 1906).

Vattel, Emer de. *The Law of Nations or the Principles of Natural Law.* Washington: The Carnegie Institute of Washington, 1916.

Walden, Chapter 1, *Writings,* Riverside edition, 11 vols. (Boston, 1893-1894).

Walker, Felix. *Felix Walker's Narrative of His Trip with Boone from Long Island to Boonesborough in March 1775.* Debow's Review of February, 1854.

Wallis, Michael. *The Real Wild West: The 101 Ranch and the Creation of the American West.* New York: St. Martin's Press, 1999.

Walter O'Meara, *Daughters of the Country: The Women of the Fur Traders and Mountain Men* (New York, 1968).

Ward, John William. *Andrew Jackson—Symbol for an Age.* London: Oxford University Press, 1953.

Ward, John William. *Andrew Jackson—Symbol for an Age.* London: Oxford University Press, 1953.
Goodrich, Charles A. *History of the United States of America.* New York: 1829.

Ward, Matthew. *Breaking The Backcountry: The Seven Years' War In Virginia And Pennsylvania 1754-1765,* University of Pittsburgh Press; 1 edition (October 17, 2004).

Washington, George, "The Creative Forces in Westward Expansion: Henderson and Boone," *American Historical Review, 20* (October 1914).

Webber, Charles Wilkins. *The Hunter-naturalist: Romance of Sporting Or, Wild Scenes and Wild Hunters.* 1852.

White, Stewart Edward, *Daniel Boone Wilderness Scout.* New York: Doubleday & Company, Inc, 1922.

Whitman, Walt. "Poem of the Sayers of the Words of the Earth," *Leaves of Grass.* (New York, 1856).

Wigglesworth, Michael. "God's Controversy with New England," in Proceedings of the Massachusetts Historical Society, XII (1871-1873).

William Gilmore Simms, "Daniel Boone—The First Hunter of Kentucky," in his *Views and Reviews in American Literature, History and Fiction,* ed. C. Hugh Holman (1845; reprint, Cambridge: Belknap Press of Harvard University, 1963).

Williams, Paul. *Jackson, Crockett, and Houston on the American Frontier.* Jefferson: McFarland & Company, Inc., 2016.

Williams, Stanley T. "The Founding of Main Street: The Letters of Mrs. Trollope," in *The North American Review,* Volume 215. New York: North American Review Corporation, 1922.

Wilson, James. *The Earth Shall Weep: A History of Native America,* New York: Atlantic Monthly Press, 1998.

Woods, M.B. Letter to Lyman Draper, April 9, 1883, *Draper Manuscripts* 4C26.

Xenophon, "On Hunting" in *Selections*. H. G. Dakyns.